A Contrastive Study of Responsibility
for Understanding Utterances between Japanese and Korean

Hituzi Linguistics in English

No.5	Communicating Skills of Intention	Tsutomu Sakamoto
No.6	A Pragmatic Approach to the Generation and Gender Gap in Japanese Politeness Strategies	Toshihiko Suzuki
No.7	Japanese Women's Listening Behavior in Face-to-face Conversation	Sachie Miyazaki
No.8	An Enterprise in the Cognitive Science of Language	Tetsuya Sano et al.
No.9	Syntactic Structure and Silence	Hisao Tokizaki
No.10	The Development of the Nominal Plural Forms in Early Middle English	Ryuichi Hotta
No.11	Chunking and Instruction	Takayuki Nakamori
No.12	Detecting and Sharing Perspectives Using Causals in Japanese	Ryoko Uno
No.13	Discourse Representation of Temporal Relations in the So-Called Head-Internal Relatives	Kuniyoshi Ishikawa
No.14	Features and Roles of Filled Pauses in Speech Communication	Michiko Watanabe
No.15	Japanese Loanword Phonology	Masahiko Mutsukawa
No.16	Derivational Linearization at the Syntax-Prosody Interface	Kayono Shiobara
No.17	Polysemy and Compositionality	Tatsuya Isono
No.18	fMRI Study of Japanese Phrasal Segmentation	Hideki Oshima
No.19	Typological Studies on Languages in Thailand and Japan	Tadao Miyamoto et al.
No.20	Repetition, Regularity, Redundancy	Yasuyo Moriya
No.21	A Cognitive Pragmatic Analysis of Nominal Tautologies	Naoko Yamamoto
No.22	A Contrastive Study of Responsibility for Understanding Utterances between Japanese and Korean	Sumi Yoon

Hituzi Linguistics in English No. 22

A Contrastive Study of Responsibility for Understanding Utterances between Japanese and Korean

Sumi Yoon

Hituzi Syobo Publishing

Copyright © Sumi Yoon 2014
First published 2014

Author: Sumi Yoon

All rights reserved. Except for the quotation of short passages for the purposes of criticism and review, no part of this publication may be reproduced, stored in a retrieval system, or transmitted in any form or by any means, electronic, mechanical, photocopying, recording or otherwise, without the written prior permission of the publisher.
In case of photocopying and electronic copying and retrieval from network personally, permission will be given on receipts of payment and making inquiries. For details please contact us through e-mail. Our e-mail address is given below.

Hituzi Syobo Publishing
Yamato bldg. 2F, 2-1-2 Sengoku Bunkyo-ku Tokyo, Japan
112-0011

phone +81-3-5319-4916 fax +81-3-5319-4917
e-mail: toiawase@hituzi.co.jp
http://www.hituzi.co.jp/
postal transfer 00120-8-142852

ISBN978-4-89476-685-3
Printed in Japan

Acknowledgements

The research described in this book, which I undertook for my doctoral degree at Kanazawa University, was supported by a number of people and institutions, and I cannot express in words the depth of my gratitude to them. First of all, I would like to express my deepest gratitude to Prof. Yoshinori Nishijima for his extraordinary support. My interest in linguistics has only grown throughout my master's and doctoral program because of his teachings, patience, and enthusiasm. I am honored to have him as my mentor. I would like to express my sincere appreciation to Profs. Kazuo Katoh, Sangyoung Nam, and Yoshimitsu Ozaki for giving me helpful guidance and having informative discussions. Dr. Sohee shin is appreciated for helping with statistical analysis. I also wish to thank my colleagues who gave me valuable comments and help at Kanazawa University. Special thanks go to the participants of this research. It would never have come into being without their generous cooperation.

I would like to acknowledge the Japan Society for the Promotion of Science for financially supporting the publication of this book. Field work in Washington, D. C. and Boston in the US, and Seoul in South Korea was supported by the K. U. (Kanazawa University) Cultural-Resource Center. I also wish to say thanks to the staff at publisher Hituzi Syobo, especially Mr. Takashi Moriwaki, for their editorial support.

Last, but certainly not least, I would like to express a deep sense of gratitude to my friends and family. Special thanks go to my husband and best friend Tyler Montgomery, and my mom Sang-pil Kim for the constant assistance, encouragement, and support they have provided throughout.

Sumi Yoon

Contents

Acknowledgements   v
List of abbreviations   xi

Chapter 1 Introduction   1

    1.1 Motives of the Book   2
    1.2 Aims of the Research   3
    1.3 Outline of this Book   4

Chapter 2 Theoretical Background and Previous Studies   7

    2.1 General Account   7
    2.2 Individualizing Language Typology   7
    2.3 Writer/Speaker-Responsible and Reader/Listener-Responsible Languages   8
       2.3.1 John Hinds' Theory   8
       2.3.2 Studies Inspired by Hinds' Theory   10
    2.4 Japanese and Korean Written Discourse in Rhetoric   12
       2.4.1 Japanese and English   13
       2.4.2 Korean and English   15
       2.4.3 Japanese and Korean   17
    2.5 Contrastive Discourse Studies between Japanese and Korean   18
       2.5.1 Apologies   19
       2.5.2 Requests   20
    2.6 Pilot Study   23
    2.7 Research Questions   24
    2.8 Hypothesis   25

Chapter 3 Methodology — 27

   3.1 General Account — 27
   3.2 Experimental Design of Conversation Situations — 27
   3.3 Participants — 29
       3.3.1 University Students — 29
           3.3.1.1 Japanese and Korean University Students Who Live in Their Own Countries — 30
           3.3.1.2 Japanese and Korean University Students Who Live in the United States of America — 30
       3.3.2 Office Workers — 30
   3.4 Methods — 30
       3.4.1 University Students — 31
           3.4.1.1 Apologies — 31
           3.4.1.2 Requests — 31
       3.4.2 Office Workers — 31
           3.4.2.1 Apologies — 32
           3.4.2.2 Requests — 32
   3.5 Data Analysis — 32
       3.5.1 Quantitative Analysis — 32
       3.5.2 Qualitative Analysis — 33

Chapter 4 Apology Discourse by Japanese and Korean University Students — 35

   4.1 General Account — 35
   4.2 Introduction — 35
   4.3 Data Analysis — 36
   4.4 Results — 38
       4.4.1 The First Turn of Apologetic Discourse — 38
       4.4.2 The Second Turn of Apologetic Discourse — 41
       4.4.3 The Third Turn of Apologetic Discourse — 43
   4.5 Discussion — 44
       4.5.1 Explanations for Apology Preferred by Korean Students — 44
       4.5.2 Expressions of Apology and Thanks — 48
       4.5.3 Influence of Daily Use of English in Responsibility for

	Understanding Utterances	48
4.6	Conclusions	51

Chapter 5 Request Discourse by Japanese and Korean University Students 53

5.1	General Account	53
5.2	Introduction	53
5.3	Data Analysis	54
5.4	Results	55
	5.4.1 The First Turn of Request-type Discourse	56
	5.4.2 The Second Turn of Request-type Discourse	56
5.5	Discussion	61
5.6	Conclusions	63

Chapter 6 Apology Discourse by Japanese and Korean Office Workers 65

6.1	General Account	65
6.2	Introduction	65
6.3	Data Analysis	66
6.4	Results	67
	6.4.1 Comparison between Japanese and Korean Office Workers	67
	6.4.2 Comparison between Japanese Female and Male Office Workers	68
	6.4.3 Comparison between Korean Female and Male Office Workers	70
6.5	Discussion	73
	6.5.1 Difference of Total Amount of Information by Japanese and Korean Office Workers	73
	6.5.2 Correlation between the Total Amount of Information and the Relationship between the Speaker and Listener	75
	6.5.3 Correlation between Total Amount of Information and Speaker's Gender	77
6.6	Conclusions	77

Chapter 7 Request Discourse by Japanese and Korean Office Workers — 79

    7.1 General Account — 79
    7.2 Introduction — 79
    7.3 Data Analysis — 80
    7.4 Results — 82
        7.4.1 Total Amount of Information by Japanese and Korean in Requests — 82
            7.4.1.1 Comparison between Japanese and Korean Office Workers — 82
            7.4.1.2 Comparison between Japanese Female and Male Office Workers — 84
            7.4.1.3 Comparison between Korean Female and Male Office Workers — 86
        7.4.2 Sentence Types of Utterances in Requests between Japanese and Korean — 88
    7.5 Discussion — 89
    7.6 Conclusions — 93

Chapter 8 Conclusions — 95

    References — 99
    Appendices — 105
    Index — 113

List of abbreviations

The Hepburn system is used for Japanese and the Yale system is used for Korean in this book.

JU: Japanese university students who live in Japan
KU: Korean university students who live in Korea
JIU: Japanese international university students who live in the U.S.
KIU: Korean international university students who live in the U.S.
JMU: Japanese male university students
JFU: Japanese female university students
KMU: Korean male university students
KFU: Korean female university students
MU: Male university students
FU: Female university students
M: Male speakers
F: Female speakers
B: Boss
C: Colleague
S: Subordinate

Chapter 1

Introduction

In this era of increasing globalization, it has become commonplace that people with culturally different backgrounds interact. In such situations, speaking a common language is not enough. It is also important to know how to use language in a culturally sensitive way because unexpected communicative behavior can bring feelings of strangeness to the conversation rather than commonality. Generally, people think that there are not many differences in communicative behavior cross-culturally, but this is not the case.

In regards to communicative behavior, there is a large body of intercultural communication research comparing Western and Asian language use. However, past research has focused less on the differences between Japanese and Korean than between English and Japanese or English and Korean, especially by Western researchers. This may be due to the fact that Japan and Korea share many similarities linguistically, culturally, geographically, economically, and historically. However, it has been found that there are constant misunderstandings and linguistic frictions between Japanese and Korean people.

It is expected that such communicative misunderstandings will increase between Japanese and Korean people. Today, Korean TV dramas, pop music, idols, and stars are currently riding a wave of popularity in Japan: the Korean Wave. It is well known that one of the reasons for the dramatic increase of Japanese learners of the Korean language since the early 2000s is the Wave (Nam, 2009). On the other hand, in Korea Japanese language has been gaining in popularity for a long time. Hence there will be more chances for Japanese and Korean people to communicate; to know and fully understand the differences between Japanese and Korean language and culture is extremely important.

1.1   Motives of the Book

From the point of view of language typology, Japanese and Korean are regarded as very similar. Both languages belong to the group of agglutinative languages, are categorized as SOV languages, and the subject and object in a sentence in both languages are not obligatory. Furthermore, the two languages have their own honorific systems no matter how they are different in relative or absolute use. In this way, Japanese and Korean are similar with respect to grammatical structure and honorific behavior.

Indeed, learning Japanese as a foreign language is easier for Korean native speakers compared to learners from other countries, especially at the beginner level. However, Korean learners of the Japanese language also find difficulties in communicating with Japanese native speakers even if they speak Japanese perfectly. This may be caused by the differences in discourse style, especially spoken discourse, between Japanese and Korean people. One is apt to think that a Korean person who speaks fluent Japanese has no problems with communicating in Japanese. However, to know Japanese vocabulary and grammar does not always mean they will be good communicators. Assumptions by language experts that Korean and Japanese are linguistically and culturally similar may account for the dearth of research comparing and contrasting both languages.

An example of these assumptions can be found in Hinds' typology of language in discourse level, where Japanese and Korean are both considered to be reader/listener-responsible languages, whereas English is classified as a writer/speaker-responsible language (Hinds, 1987). Considering common rhetorical features of both languages, Japanese and Korean have been understood to be listener-responsible languages in discourse. However, on the conversational level, I demonstrated that Korean should be classified as a speaker-responsible language based on my contrastive analysis of daily conversations between married couples in Japanese and Korean, where address terms are used as *contextualization cues* (Gumperz, 1982) to convey a speaker's intention to the interlocutor metacommunicatively (Yoon, 2009). Furthermore, it was also pointed out that Korean couples use address terms as *contextualization cues* more frequently and more variously than Japanese couples, especially in apologies and requests.

1.2   Aims of the Research

This research examines different communication styles in terms of the responsibility for understanding utterances (Hinds, 1987) on the conversational level between Japanese and Korean. The hypothesis is that Japanese is a listener-responsible language in which the speakers give less information and use unclear expressions, thus the responsibility for understanding utterances falls on the listener, while Korean should be categorized as a speaker-responsible language, in which the speaker is actively responsible for the listener's understanding of utterances (Yoon, 2009)[1].

In order to demonstrate the hypothesis, the total amount of information as well as the types of utterances by Japanese and Korean speakers was analyzed. The correlations between the responsibility for understanding utterances and the relationship between the speaker and the listener were analyzed using responses taken from Korean and Japanese office workers in predefined scenarios. Furthermore, responses from Japanese and Korean university students who live in their own countries and who live in the United States of America were analyzed. The analysis focused on the roles of the speaker's native language and gender, the relationship between the speaker and the listener, and the influence of the daily use of English on the responsibility for the understanding of utterances. There are four general aims of this study:

> 1) To draw attention to the differences between written discourse and spoken discourse from the point of view of responsibility for the understanding of text and utterances, through the reconsideration of Hinds' theory that both Japanese and Korean are categorized as reader/listener-responsible languages;
> 2) to demonstrate that Japanese is a listener-responsible language while Korean is a speaker-responsible language on the conversational level, even though they have very similar linguistic and cultural features;
> 3) to contribute to the development of contrastive research between Japanese and Korean in regards to the responsibility for the understanding of utterances;
> 4) to suggest implications of this research on second-language acquisition and on intercultural communication between Japanese and Korean speakers.

1.3 Outline of this Book

This book consists of eight chapters including the present chapter.

In Chapter 2, the theoretical background of the theme of responsibility for understanding utterances and previous contrastive studies of Japanese and Korean discourse, especially with respect to apologies and requests, are discussed. The claim of Hinds (1987) which suggested a new typology of languages (writer/speaker-responsible vs. reader/listener-responsible languages) and asserted that both Japanese and Korean are reader/listener-responsible languages with respect to the responsibility for the understanding of discourse, is also reviewed and reconsidered in order to formulate a hypothesis of this study.

Chapter 3 describes in detail the methodology and methods and materials used to survey Japanese and Korean university students and office workers.

Chapters 4 and 5 analyze the differences in responsibility for understanding utterances between Japanese and Korean speakers. They also deal with how the daily use of English by native Japanese and Korean university students influences the responsibility for the understanding of utterances in their native language.

Chapters 6 and 7 present the results of research on Japanese and Korean office workers with regards to the total amount of information and sentence types in apologies and requests, and confirm the results of Chapters 4 and 5. The correlations between the responsibility for understanding of utterances and the relationships between the speaker and listener are discussed in Chapters 6 and 7.

Chapter 8 discusses the concept of responsibility for the understanding of utterances, Hinds' theory, and differences between Japanese and Korean on the conversational level. Finally, the implications of this research for second language acquisition of Japanese and Korean and intercultural communication are considered.

Endnotes

1 The difference of utterances between Japanese and Korean can also be explained from the point view of explicity, however, the responsibility for understanding utterances can be captured more adequately from an interactional perspective. Therefore, the responsibility for

understanding utterances has to be determined not only qualitatively, but also quantitatively.

Chapter 2

Theoretical Background and Previous Studies

2.1 General Account

In this chapter, the theoretical background of the present research and previous associated studies are described and some criticisms of the studies are suggested. First, the language typology of Hinds (1987) that classified languages with respect to responsibility for understanding discourse into writer/speaker-responsible and reader/listener-responsible categories, and some studies that were inspired by Hinds' typology are introduced. Second, previous studies with reference to comparisons between Japanese and Korean in apologies and requests are reviewed. Finally, the research questions of the present study are addressed.

2.2 Individualizing Language Typology

Ikegami (2000) surveyed three approaches in terms of language typology by quoting Greenberg (1974) as follows:

    1) Generalizing Typology;
    2) Classifying Typology;
    3) Individualizing Typology.

    1) Generalizing Typology and 2) Classifying Typology are two different internal orientations in modern language typology suggested by Greenberg (1974). On the other hand, Ikegami (2000) described that 3) Individualizing

Typology is a field that attempts to characterize a language by distinguishing it from other languages.

Horie & Pardeshi (2009) claimed that Cognitive Typology and Individualizing Typology are almost the same by citing Ikegami (2000). Horie & Pardeshi (2009) also pointed out that the slight differences between Japanese and Korean, which have a lot in common with reference to typology, share similarities culturally and socially, and have a lot of contact with each other, are very interesting from the point of view of Cognitive Typology.

The present research attempts to compare two languages, Japanese and Korean, in terms of responsibility for understanding utterances (speaker-responsible and listener-responsible) based on Individualizing Typology. Only Japanese and Korean are considered subjects in the present research[1].

2.3 Writer/Speaker-Responsible and Reader/Listener-Responsible Languages

2.3.1 John Hinds' Theory

Hinds (1987) claimed that languages can be categorized as reader/listener-responsible or writer/speaker-responsible, and pointed out that English is a writer/speaker-responsible language and Japanese and Korean are both reader/listener-responsible languages because of the similarity of writing patterns. He states:

> In Japan, perhaps in Korea, and certainly in Ancient China, there is a different way of looking at the communication process. In Japan, it is the responsibility of the listener (or reader) to understand what it is that the speaker or author had intended to say. (Hinds, 1987: 144)

As he used the word *perhaps*, it might be assumed that both Japanese and Korean are classified as listener-responsible languages without any analysis of the data on the conversational level, solely based on research of an essay written in English and Japanese. He also simply introduced an episode associated with speaker-responsibility and listener-responsibility between an American woman and a Japanese taxi driver by citing Naotsuka & Sakamoto *et al.* (1981) as follows:

> An American woman was taking a taxi to the Ginza Tokyu Hotel. The taxi driver mistakenly took her to the Ginza Daiichi Hotel. She said "I'm

sorry, I should have spoken more clearly." This, I take to be an indication of her speaker-responsible upbringing. The taxi driver demonstrated his listener-responsible background when he replied, "No, no, I should have listened more carefully." (Hinds, 1987: 144)

It is also possible to assume that the American woman apologized for what she had said because her Japanese pronunciation may not have been clear enough if they talked to each other in Japanese. Conversely, the taxi driver may have apologized to the woman, even though he thought it was not his fault, because she was a customer. In general, it is hard to imagine that a taxi driver in Japan would insist in front of the customer that he was right. Thus, to demonstrate which language is speaker-responsible or listener-responsible, clearly defined, objective situations should be examined. For example, a conversation by a speaker and a listener who are from the same country, are the same age or social status, and speak the same language should be observed.

Hinds (1987) examined an expository essay from the Asahi Shimbun's daily column *Tensei Jingo* ('Vox Populi, Vox Dei') and its English translation and found two main reasons why Japanese should be categorized as a reader/listener-responsible language. First, in terms of rhetorical pattern Japanese essays, including the one mentioned above, are organized by *ki-sho-ten-ketsu*. In *ten*, new subtopics are introduced, but are written in a style which assumes the reader is already familiar with the subtopics. Second, Hinds (1987) noted that there was an absence or attenuation of landmarks that help the reader understand the relationship between sentences.

There are three criticisms of Hinds' theory of reader/listener responsibility vs. writer/speaker responsibility. First, it is not appropriate to compare an original Japanese column and its translated English version. The writer's expectations of the reader are different. The original column was written for Japanese readers who can understand Japanese and live in Japan, and are familiar with present Japanese society and culture. In contrast, the English version was written for people who may be Japanese but find it hard to understand Japanese language, society, or culture because they live in other countries, or who are not Japanese but are interested in Japanese language, society, or culture. Also, it should have been taken into consideration that the person who translated the Japanese column into English may or may not have been a native Japanese speaker or English speaker. If he or she was a native Japanese speaker, it is also possible that his or her Japanese was influenced by English or vice versa.

Second, Hinds used the term listener-responsible and speaker-responsible without any experimental consideration on the level of conversation except citing the episode between an American customer and a Japanese taxi driver from Naotsuka & Sakamoto *et al.* (1981) as shown above. It is possible that language has different features in regards to responsibility for understanding discourse in written texts and spoken utterances.

Third, Korean is categorized as a reader/listener-responsible language by inference that Korean language and Japanese language share common syntactic features and writing patterns. There are many studies which demonstrate the differences between Japanese and Korean discourse, although the languages are structurally very similar. Thus it is too simplistic to put Japanese and Korean in the same category without any experimental consideration.

2.3.2 Studies Inspired by Hinds' Theory

Mauranen (1993) compared texts written by Finnish and Anglo-American writers, and found differences in the expectations of the readers. She cited the distinction made by Hinds (1987) and claimed that Anglo-American writers are from a writer-responsible culture since the writers bear the main responsibility for the understanding of the text, while Finnish writers, whose writing patterns appear similar to the Japanese writers (assigning the main responsibility to readers), are from a reader-responsible culture.

Connor (1996) also discussed reader-responsibility in terms of contrastive rhetoric in different languages by citing Hinds (1987, 1990) and Eggington (1987), who said that both Japanese and Korean are reader-responsible languages compared to English.

Qi & Liu (2007) pointed out that Chinese is a reader/listener-responsible language and English is a writer/speaker-responsible language. They found that Chinese EFL (English as a Foreign Language[2]) students' English writing and those of native American English speakers are different, and Chinese students have their own writing patterns. The Chinese writers require the reader's background knowledge, while the American writers organize rhetoric logically in written discourses and do not need the reader's background knowledge.

The studies inspired by Hinds' theory have focused on English writing education and have used English writings that were written by English native speakers and non-native English speakers to examine whether they are reader-responsible or writer-responsible. The same methodological problems arise that were found in Hinds (1987): Original writings that are written by native speakers should be compared to avoid the issues pointed out in section 2.3.1.

In regards to conversational level, Horie & Pardeshi (2009) pointed out that Japanese is a listener-responsible language by citing Ogiwara (2008) as follows:

> It is assumed that Japanese people do not always consider the meaning of utterances literally. In a high-context culture[3] such as Japanese culture, the ratio between literal vs. figurative interpretation tends to be low.
>
> Ogiwara (2008: 303[4])

> As discussed by Ogiwara, in Japanese conversation, the ratio of the literal interpretation of the language vs. the figurative interpretation is low. The conversation tends to progress by monitoring the conversation and making cooperative inferences. It shows that Japanese is a listener-responsible language (Hinds, 1987).
>
> Horie & Pardeshi (2009: 82[5])

Takigawa (2006) analyzed a conversation between a Japanese wife and her American husband and found that the Japanese wife stated the point at the end of her story and her American husband had difficulty following her story. His results seem to support Hinds' *delayed introduction of purpose* (Hinds, 1990: 98) on the conversational level in Japanese. Hinds (1990) described how writing in Japanese, Chinese, Thai, and Korean favors a "quasi-inductive" rather than an inductive or a deductive style of presentation, or "delayed introduction of purpose". The "delayed introduction of purpose" makes the writing appear incoherent to the English-speaking reader. It is important to note that Takigawa (2006) attempted to demonstrate the theory of Hinds (1987; 1990) on the conversational level and found a similar result to Hinds (1990). However, Takigawa (2006) examined the responsibility for understanding utterances with a very specific example: A short Japanese conversation between an American husband who lives in Japan and speaks both Japanese and English, and his Japanese wife who had lived in the U.S. and studied English.

In the field of contrastive linguistic studies between Japanese and Korean, a few attempts have been made to clarify the responsibility for understanding utterances, though they did not cite Hinds' (1987) claims. Yim (2003) compared Japanese and Korean with respect to the responsibility of the listener for understanding utterances. According to Yim (2003), Japanese listeners are better than Korean listeners at interpreting the intentions of the speakers. However, he focused on different types of speech acts used between both languages rather than responsibility for understanding utterances.

Yim & Ide (2004) pointed out that Japanese and Korean people have different perspectives about speaking and expressing their opinions: Compared to Japanese society, Korean society is more similar to American society than Japanese society. If someone cannot convey his or her opinion clearly, many Korean listeners think that the speaker is not intelligent. Yim & Ide (2004) introduced some examples which supported their claims that Korean people insist on their point of view if a car accident happened, and utter a reason why they were late for an appointment even toward older interlocutors (Yim & Ide, 2004: 102;107).

2.4 Japanese and Korean Written Discourse in Rhetoric

There are many studies on comparative writing patterns between some East Asian languages and American English after Kaplan (1966), especially in the field of English education as a second language, though they do not focus on reader/listener responsibility or writer/reader responsibility directly. Kaplan (1966) suggests that there are different types of rhetorical organization depending on the culture or native language. By analyzing ESL (English as a Second Language) students' expository writing styles, Kaplan (1966) states that Korean and Chinese are categorized as "Oriental" cultural thought pattern (Kaplan, 1966: 10).

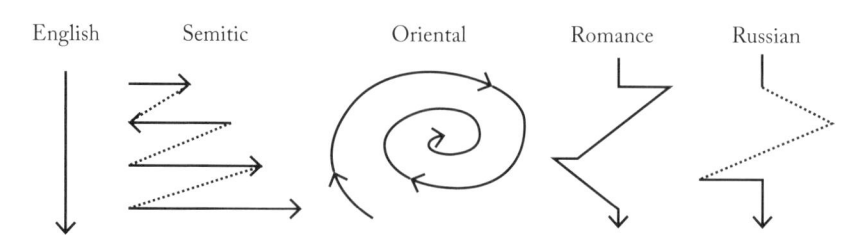

English   Semitic   Oriental   Romance   Russian

Figure 1. Visual representations of the various paragraphs by Kaplan (Kaplan, 1966: 15)

Hinds (1983) criticized Kaplan (1966). The first of his three criticisms is that the data analyzed to investigate rhetoric patterns in the study was written in English by ESL students instead of being written in their first languages. Second, Hinds pointed out that the "Oriental" pattern was over-generalized. The third criticism was concerned with the "English" pattern which was described as a straight line. Hinds claimed that English rhetoric pattern is not described by only a straight line.

Based on his analysis of an English essay and several English translations into Japanese, Chinese, Thai, and Korean, Hinds (1990) pointed out that Japanese and Korean have several common features in writing. For example, in analyzed essays the Japanese and Korean authors mentioned their purpose in the final sentences (*delayed introduction of purpose*; Hinds, 1990: 98) and therefore it is difficult for English-speaking readers to understand.

Even though there are distinct cultural differences between China, Korea, and Japan, they are considered parts of the overall East Asian culture. Furthermore, Hinds (1987, 1990) inferred that Korean rhetoric will be similar to rhetoric in Japanese, due to the shared intellectual traditions based on the influences of Confucianism, Taoism, and Buddhism (Powers and Gong, 1994). Based on the reasons above, Japanese and Korean have been categorized as not only reader-responsible languages but also listener-responsible languages.

As for indirectness between Anglo-American and Asian writings, Hinkel (1997) asserted the findings of earlier studies (Cherry, 1988; Swales, 1990) that indirectness strategies associated with spoken discourse are also employed in written academic prose (Hinkel, 1997: 381–382). The findings of Hinkel (1997) indicated that speakers of Chinese, Korean, Japanese, and Indonesian utilized rhetorical questions and tags, disclaimers and denials, vagueness and ambiguity, repetition, several types of hedges, ambiguous pronouns, and the passive voice with greater frequency than Anglo-American speakers did.

2.4.1 Japanese and English

Hinds (1983) claimed that a common organizational framework for Japanese compositions is *ki-sho-ten-ketsu* which was used in classical Chinese poetry (*chi-cheng-juan-he*) and was exported to Korea (*ki-sung-chon-kyul*) and Japan. By citing Takemata (1976), Hinds (1983) defined the *ki-sho-ten-ketsu* as follows:

- A. ki First, begin one's argument.
- B. shoo Next, develop that.
- C. ten At the point where this development is finished, turn the idea to a subtheme where there is a connection, but not a directly connected association (to the major theme).

D. ketsu   Last, bring all of this together and reach a conclusion.

(Hinds, 1983: 188)

In his study, Hinds (1983) pointed out that the organization of the Japanese essay is greatly different from English expository prose because of the presence of a sudden topic change introduced in a *ten* paragraph, and the conclusion is an indication of a doubt or a question.

Kobayashi (1984) defined two different rhetoric patterns G-S (General-to-Specific) and S-G (Specific-to-general) and claimed that American students writing in English tend to use the GS pattern, while Japanese students writing in Japanese tend to use the SG pattern. The definition of GS and SG by Kobayashi (1984) is as follows:

General-to-specific
The writing tends to have a direct relationship between the general and specific statements because it excludes irrelevant ideas. The writing tends to be performance-oriented; that is, writers seem more conscious of the need to organize their ideas for an audience.

Specific-to-general
The writing tends to have a less direct relationship between the general and specific statements because it includes specifics loosely related to the general idea. The writing tends to be process-oriented because the direction is not restricted by a general statement.   (Kobayashi, 1984: 103)

Miyake (2007) compared the narratives written in Japanese and English by Japanese students who go to university or ESL class in the U.S., and found some differences between Japanese and English writings. For example, subjects were omitted from the Japanese narratives, and Japanese sentences were longer than English sentences. Furthermore, she found that the Japanese writing style was influenced by the English writing style. Also, the length of English instruction affected the Japanese students' writing: the longer the students studied English, the better their writing became (Miyake, 2007: 73).

Kubota (1997) critically surveyed contrastive rhetoric studies which characterized Japanese expository prose as a classical style (*ki-sho-ten-ketsu*), reader responsible, and an inductive style compared to English. Four arguments were presented by Kubota (1997) as follows:

> The first argument is that language and culture need to be viewed as dynamic rather than exotic and static. Second, the claim that *ki-sho-ten-ketsu* constitutes a typical pattern for Japanese expository prose is over generalized from a small number of selected samples. Third, the multiple and often conflicting interpretations and functions of *ki-sho-ten-ketsu* offered by Japanese composition specialists bring into question the legitimacy of claiming this pattern as the typical preferred style in Japanese. Finally, a review of the development of the modern Japanese language reveals a continuous influence of English and European languages on Japanese writing. (Kubota, 1997: 462)

2.4.2 Korean and English

Studies regarding contrastive rhetoric in Korean and English have been done in the field of English as a foreign language, especially in terms of academic writing. Eggington (1987) researched Korean academic written discourse and found that Korean writers preferred the rhetorical structure of *ki-sung-chon-kyul* [introduction-development-turn-conclusion], which appears to follow the same pattern as Japanese *ki-sho-ten-ketsu* which has its origin in classical Chinese poetry (Eggington, 1987: 156). However, his analysis was based on the level of text and it is not clear whether it is also valid on the conversational level. Furthermore, in his study, Eggington (1987) claimed that Korean writers should use the English writing style because it is easier for English native speakers to understand. At the same time, some researchers have insisted that EFL teachers need to be careful not to give their students the impression that what they learned about good writing in their native country is not valued in the academic arena (Park, 2007: 205).

Park (2007) interviewed two native EFL teachers and three EFL Korean students about what they think constitute good writing. According to Park (2007), the teachers and the students agreed that good writing should be unified and clear so that readers can follow it easily. However, the students' responses indicated that Korean writers have different writing styles compared to American English writers. Park (2007) stated the reasons as follows:

> …it is likely that Korean students see a piece of writing that compels the reader to discover the text's message through subtle hints left by the writer as good academic writing simply because that sort of writing serves as a model

in Korean textbooks and assessments. This might, in turn, lead the student to assume that it is the reader who is responsible for clear communication rather than the writer. (Park, 2007: 198)

As Park (2007) pointed out, Korean people are educated at institutions such as junior high schools or high schools on how to write good prose, in which the author's intention is hidden in the text. In other words, Korean people consider prose in which it is not easy to understand the real purpose to be high quality prose.

Burke (2010) surveyed some characteristics of the construction of writing identities by Korean ESL undergraduate and graduate students. Burke (2010) confirmed the claim of Kubota (1997) that writers' identities are multiple, shifted, and conflicted. The process of the construction is dynamic and varies individually. Also, writer identities in social, textual, and discourse aspects do not always match one another. Not only do their native language and culture influence identity, but also their attitude and goals in the level of the program become influential factors in constructing academic writers' identities (Burke, 2010: 317).

Three critical questions arise about previous studies on contrastive rhetoric and written discourse studies. First, research on contrastive writing rhetoric or composition, including the studies above, especially in the field of ESL or EFL writing pedagogy has focused on differences between English and other languages written in English (Leki, 1997). However, to compare two or more languages, the original untranslated writing should be analyzed to prevent translation errors from affecting the research. For example, it is usually known that Japanese and Korean speakers use personal pronouns such as "I" or "we" as a subject in English academic writing because Japanese and Korean students are not familiar with using inanimate norms as a subject (Park, 2007). Ironically, Japanese and Korean speakers do not use personal pronouns frequently in Japanese or Korean academic writings, since it is possible to omit the subject in Japanese and Korean. Therefore, to demonstrate the differences between two or more languages, the original versions should be compared to each other.

Second, both Japanese and Korean are categorized as part of the group of oriental or East Asian languages (Kaplan 1966; Connor, 1996; Hinkel, 1997; Hinds, 1990). No matter how Japanese and Korean languages are similar or share common historic cultural features, Japanese and Korean language, culture, society, and people are different. Japanese and Korean should be treated and examined as independent languages.

Third, even though written discourse and spoken discourse should be considered separately, it was assumed that both Japanese and Korean people will speak in the same way: indirectly, expecting that their interlocutors can understand the real purpose of the utterances, because Japanese and Korean share some similar rhetoric factors (Hinds, 1987; 1990; Hinkel 1997).

As Kubota (1997) pointed out, Japanese writing style has been changed by the influence of Western culture. Not only have Japanese and Korean writing styles changed but also their speaking styles have changed. This is especially true since the Korean government started emphasizing learning English in public education. Western culture has become strongly embedded in Korean education and traditional Confucius literature and as a result Korean language education has been neglected to some extent (Burke, 2010: 69). There is also a phrase reflecting Korean parents' passion for their children's English education: *Kileki appa (goose father)*, which refers to the recent phenomenon of fathers living in Korea by themselves and sending money to their wives and children who live abroad to study English. The number of *goose fathers* has been increasing steadily for the last 20 years.

2.4.3 Japanese and Korean

There have been few contrastive studies of Japanese and Korean that have focused on rhetoric or the compositional structure of prose (Sugita, 1994; Kim & Maeda, 1997; Lee, 2001; 2008; Seo & Yanagisawa, 2007) since both languages have been considered very similar in terms of writing pattern (Eggington 1987; Hinds 1987; 1990; Kaplan 1966).

In terms of compositional structure, the differences between Japanese and Korean were demonstrated by Kim & Maeda (1997). Kim & Maeda (1997) compared compositions which were written by Japanese and Korean university students. The students were asked to write a composition based on four picture story cards shown by the researchers. Kim & Maeda (1997) claimed that Japanese writers tried to end the story with an unexpected humorous twist by switching the order of the number 3 and number 4 cards (so that the order of the story is 1–2–4–3), while Korean writers made the story using the 1–2–3–4 order of the cards. It was also found that Korean writers gave more information in their writing than Japanese writers.

In terms of contrastive rhetoric between Japanese and Korean, Lee (2008) and Seo & Yanagisawa (2007) analyzed the editorials of Japanese and Korean newspapers from Japan and Korea. Lee (2008) claimed that there are differences between Japanese and Korean rhetoric patterns even though there are many commonalities on the sentence level. The results of Lee (2008) showed that the sentences which describe the Japanese writers' purpose are located in the last part of the editorials. Conversely, the purpose of the writers is found in the first part of the Korean editorials.

Lee (2008) also focused on the differences in the beginning sentences in Japanese and Korean editorials, since the beginning sentence influences the editorials' tone (Ichikawa, 1971 cited by Lee, 2008). According to Lee (2008), two differences were clarified. First, Japanese editorials tend to handle the contents objectively, by describing facts of the subject. On the other hand, Korean editorials tend to handle the contents subjectively, including judgments or opinions of the editors about the subject. Second, assertive forms are used in predicates for the beginning sentences in most Korean editorials, while the forms are not used in Japanese editorials.

Also, similar results have been found with different rhetoric patterns in Japanese and Korean editorials by Seo & Yanagisawa (2007). According to Seo & Yanagisawa (2007), in Korean editorials the writers tend to convey their opinion with coherence, while Japanese editorial writers try to convey their prudence and combined sights by using subordinate conjunctions frequently.

These results are very important because they demonstrate that Japanese and Korean rhetoric patterns are different even though they had been considered to be similar in early studies. In addition, both Japanese and Korean writings are written by native Japanese and Korean, and analyzed directly in order to compare differences between the two languages. They are also different from early studies which analyzed the English writings written by native speakers and non-native speakers, or different types of writings between subject languages.

2.5 Contrastive Discourse Studies between Japanese and Korean

This section discusses previous studies which analyzed apologies and requests in order to compare the differences in utterances by Japanese and Korean speakers.

Two speech acts, apologies and requests, both constitute *face-threatening acts* (Brown and Levinson, 1987), and both speech acts were chosen for the present study because they are related to events that are costly to the listener (Blum-Kulka *et al.*, 1989). In other words, apologies and requests are important in the field of intercultural communication because the degree of imposition changes depending on the language[6]. However, little attention has been paid to Japanese and Korean in the field of contrastive linguistics. This is especially true of apologies, since it is easy to assume that there is less conflict between Japanese and Korean in communication because of the cultural, linguistic, and geographic similarities they share.

2.5.1 Apologies

Previous contrastive work on apologies between Japanese and Korean was done by Ogoshi (1993). In the study, she pointed out that the different ways of grasping the relationship between the speaker and listener reflected apology expressions in Japanese and Korean, even though both languages are very similar with reference to language construction and expression. Compared to English, the border between apology and thanks expressions is unclear in both Japanese and Korean. In other words, apologetic expressions in Japanese and Korean are used in thankful situations and vice versa. Also, Ogoshi (1993) analyzed original Japanese novels and the Korean translations as well as original Korean novels and the Japanese translations. According to her analysis, two expressions ("Coysonghamnita", "Mianhamnita") are used for apologies in Korean, while three expressions ("Sumimasen", "Moshiwakegozaimasen", and "Gomennasai") are used in Japanese.

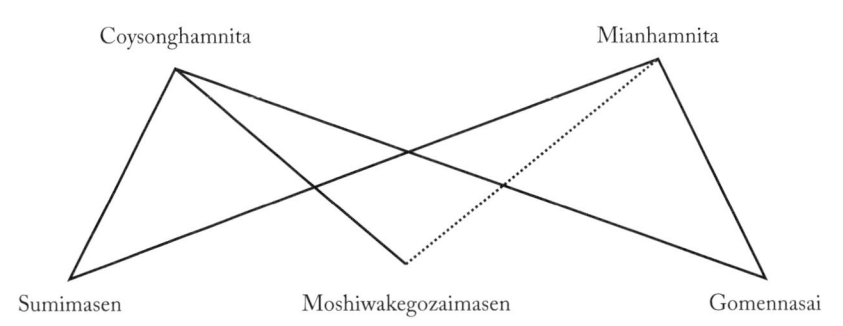

Figure 2 Correspondence between Japanese and Korean apology expressions

(Ogoshi, 1993: 32)

As shown in Figure 2, Ogoshi (1993) pointed out that the Korean apology expression "Coysonghamnita" can be translated into the Japanese apology expressions "Sumimasen", "Moshiwakegozaimasen" and "Gomennasai". However, the Korean phrase "Mianhamnita" can be translated directly into the Japanese phrases "Sumimasen" and "Gomennasai" but not into "Moshiwakegozaimasen".

In terms of apology expressions, Hong (2006) compared Japanese and Korean speakers' apology speech behavior by creating a situation where the subjects step on someone's foot on the subway by accident. He claimed that the Korean apology expressions "Coysonghamnita" and "Mianhamnita" are equivalent to the Japanese apology expressions "Sumimasen" and "Gomennasai", respectively, because the rate of use of the expressions is similar.

Kim (1996) focused not only on apology expressions but also on the use of adverbs or explanations, and found that Korean speakers used adverbs for apology expression more frequently compared to Japanese, and that the use of adverbs depends on the degree of apology. For example, Korean speakers use adverbs more frequently in serious apology situations.

According to Jin (2004), there is no difference in the use of standard expressions by Japanese and Korean speakers in apology situations in which a speaker harms or causes trouble for a listener. However, there are some differences between Japanese and Korean expressions if there is a relationship between the speaker and the listener in less serious apology situations: Japanese speakers tend to view the situation as an apology situation and utter a standard apology expression, while Korean speakers do not view the same situation as an apology situation.

2.5.2 Requests

In this section, previous contrastive studies which focus on requests in Japanese and Korean, are classified into four groups depending on what the studies introduce and reconsider. First, some previous studies have focused on comparing sentence types or expressions of requests (Ogoshi, 1995; Mo, 2001; Son, 2005 C. Kim, 2006; Lim & Tamaoka, 2010) and second, some studies have focused on strategies such as using semantic formulas (Sasakawa, 1999; Eom, 2001; Byon, 2004; Yoo, 2008; Oki *et al.*, 2009). Third, several studies have compared Japanese spoken by native Japanese speakers and Korean Japanese learners and vice versa in terms of pedagogical implications (Cho, 1997; Tsuchida, 2003; J. Kim, 2006; Wada *et al*, 2010; Kim, 2011). Finally, Ozaki (2008) compared the behavior of making requests depending on the speakers' and listeners' relationship or the weight of a request by Japanese and Korean speakers.

Ogoshi (1995) compared request expressions in Japanese and Korean and claimed that both Japanese and Korean use different types of interrogative, imperative, or other types of sentences depending on the situation and their relationship with the interlocutors in requests. Similarly, C. Kim (2006) overviewed how requests are referred to in Japanese and Korean, and pointed out that indirect expression rather than direct expressions are usually used out of consideration for the feelings of the interlocutor in Japanese requests. In contrast, Korean speakers tend to use direct expressions to convey the contents of the utterances clearly to the interlocutors.

Eom (2001) compared Japanese and Korean with respect to the amount of explanations used in requests by Japanese and Korean speakers and found that Japanese speakers uttered explanations more than Korean speakers. The result of Eom (2001) is opposite to the result of Wada *et al.* (2010) who demonstrated that the amount of information given is related to the speaker's situation, and Korean speakers gave explanations for reasons more than Japanese speakers. Explanation includes 'apology' and Eom (2001) found that Japanese speakers used apology expressions more than Korean speakers, while Korean speakers used 'suggestion', 'promise', and 'compensation' more than Japanese speakers. Eom (2001) claimed that requests by Korean speakers are similar to those by American speakers by citing Kawanari (1993). It is necessary to closely examine the amount of information in requests by Japanese and Korean speakers since the results of previous studies are contradictory.

Ozaki (2008) examined the differences in request speech behavior by Japanese and Korean speakers by setting two different degrees of situations in request: asking a person who is going to the post office to send a letter, and asking a person who is going out to buy a book but was not originally going to the store. According to Ozaki (2008), there are no particular differences in requests by Japanese and Korean speakers generally, especially if the degree of the request was not high. However, it was found that Korean people used requests more than Japanese with their friends or family members when the degree of the request was high, and he claimed that this difference will be a key point for inter-cultural communication between Japanese and Korean speakers, even though the difference between Japanese and Korean requests was not large (Ozaki, 2008: 194).

Yoo (2008) investigated whether the use of strategies in requests is different in Japanese and Korean. Yoo (2008) reported that Japanese and Korean have both common and different strategic expressions. Both Japanese and Korean speakers used the strategic expressions reason, request, and thanks. Apology and finishing[7] were used by Japanese speakers more than Korean speakers, while compensation and securing were used by Korean speakers more than Japanese speakers. Japanese speakers used strategic expressions after accepting the requests, but Korean speakers uttered strategic expressions before the listeners' accepted. Yoo (2008) claimed that it is important to show the differences between the languages to Japanese students who study Korean as a second language and vice versa.

Oki *et al.* (2009) compared Japanese and Korean cultural attitudes and language used in requests by analyzing Japanese and Korean communications in which graduate students request a letter of recommendation for a scholarship from their professors. It was pointed out that Japanese speakers tend not to verbalize the contents and reasons for their requests, and leave the inference and contents of the reasons to their interlocutors. Conversely, Korean speakers frequently uttered their reasons for the request to the interlocutor actively in Korean. This supported the results of Yoo (2008) in terms of the use of finishing expressions, for example "Yoroshiku onegaishimasu" (Well, please take care of the matter.); Japanese speakers uttered these more than Korean speakers.

There are some pedagogical studies in relation to requests by Japanese and Korean speakers which focused on the acquisition of Japanese as a second language (Cho, 1997; Tsuchida, 2003; Matsuda *et al.*, 2007; Wada *et al.*, 2010; Kim, 2011). The differences between the Japanese spoken by native Japanese and the Japanese spoken by Korean speakers in requests were examined, because the latter is influenced by Korean language and Korean discourse.

In terms of politeness, Japanese native speakers prefaced request expressions by saying "Could you do me a favor?" more than Korean Japanese language learners when the interlocutor is not intimate with the speaker (Tsuchida, 2003). Korean learners of the Japanese language were not as effective in expressing "Onegaishitemo yoroshiidesuka" to an intimate person compared to a person who was not as intimate (Cho, 1997). Whether the interlocutor was older or not, Japanese native speakers used the same request expressions toward their family. However, Korean learners used request expressions differently depending on their status in the family (J. Kim, 2006). Korean Japanese language learners felt more pressure when they made a request of a person of higher status or an older person compared to Japanese speakers in a similar situation (Wada *et al.*, 2010).

Kim (2011) compared Japanese native speakers and Korean Japanese learners to find out how different their requests strategies are in similar recommendation situations as Oki *et al.* (2009) above. According to Kim (2011), Japanese native speakers provided more information about the necessity of the recommendation after uttering the explanation of the situation, while Korean Japanese learners tended not to utter those as much and used direct request expressions instead. In terms of providing information or explanation, the results of Kim (2011) are opposite from those of Oki *et al.* (2009) which compared Japanese and Korean, spoken by Japanese and Korean native speakers, respectively.

As for sentence types of requests, Mo (2001) claimed that indirect expressions are used to build a relationship of trust by finding mutual ground, and to narrow the distance between the speaker and listener in Korean. However, these expressions may sound too strong or pushy if translated directly into Japanese. J. Kim (2006) found that Korean learners of Japanese frequently used "~te kudasai", a direct Japanese expression for request, toward a higher status person, while Japanese native speakers did not. Korean Japanese learners used the expression because "~te kudasai" is similar to the Korean expression "~e/a cuseyyo" and it can be used toward a higher status person in Korean.

As shown above, most of the studies focusing on contrastive Japanese and Korean apologies and requests have focused on differences in proper expressions, strategies, and behavior but not on the responsibility for the understanding of utterances. However, the results of some previous studies have shown that Korean speakers give more information than Japanese speakers (Matsuda *et al.*, 2007), and Korean speakers use more direct expressions such as "~ e/a cuseyyo (please do something)" (Ogoshi, 1995; C. Kim, 2006; Mo, 2001) in requests which is interesting in respect to the purpose of this study.

2.6 Pilot Study

I collected results from experimental conversations by Japanese and Korean married couples in order to examine differences in regards to the responsibility for understanding utterances in both languages (Yoon, 2009). The participants of the pilot study were nine Japanese and ten Korean married couples in their 20's and 30's, living in the capital spheres of Tokyo and Seoul, respectively, and junior college or university educated. The participants verbally reacted to the role play situations set up by the researcher. The conversations were recorded and transcribed.

In terms of the amount of information, the results showed that all the Japanese husbands uttered only an apology expression, while Korean husbands added the reasons for apologizing. I claimed that Japanese husbands expected their wives to understand their feelings even without an explanation (Yoon, 2009). On the other hand, Korean husbands explained their reasons for apologizing actively so that their wives could understand their feelings.

In terms of the types of utterances, Japanese wives tended to utter their opinions as tag questions to request an agreement with their husbands rather than to announce an intention, while all Korean wives uttered their request directly. They did not use any weakness in their expressions, unlike the Japanese wives. In other words, Japanese wives used rhetorical questions as indirect forms of expressing their opinions.

I found that Korean speakers utter more directly and clearly, give more information than Japanese speakers to convey their intention and do not need the cooperation of their listeners (Yoon, 2009). On the other hand, the Japanese speakers utter more indirectly and less clearly, give less information and expect active cooperation by the listeners. To summarize, Korean speakers are mainly responsible for the understanding of utterances and lead the communication, while the Japanese speakers will lead the communication passively and listeners are expected to interpret the intention of the speaker actively.

The results above do not support Hinds' theory (Hinds, 1987), which stated that Japanese and Korean are both listener-responsible languages. These results also suggest that Japanese and Korean are different in regards to the responsibility for the understanding of utterances: Japanese is a listener-responsible language and Korean is a speaker-responsible language. In the present study, therefore, the suggestions will be examined by focusing on the amount of information and sentences types uttered by Japanese and Korean speakers in a large sample.

2.7   Research Questions

Japanese and Korean are very similar in their linguistic structure and both Japan and Korea share common backgrounds culturally, historically, economically, and geographically. Thus, Japanese and Korean are usually classified under the same category, especially by Western researchers. As described above, Hinds (1987) categorized both Japanese and Korean as listener-responsible languages compared to English which is categorized as a speaker-responsible language, in regards to understanding utterances. Many researchers support Hinds' claim (Eggington, 1987; Connor, 1996; Hinkel, 1997) by focusing on written discourse in both languages. However, several studies have shown that there are different patterns or features in Japanese and Korean written discourse (Sugita, 1994; Kim & Maeda, 1997; Seo & Yanagisawa, 2007; Lee, 2008). Also, it was found in the pilot study (Yoon, 2009) that Japanese and Korean are different in terms of responsibility for the understanding of utterances on the conversational level.

After a thorough review of past research concerning responsibility for understanding utterances, four general research questions arise and will be addressed:

(1) Are Japanese and Korean really both listener-responsible languages since it was found that they have similar rhetorical features which are described as nonlinear or have indirect development of themes?
(2) Is the amount of information uttered different between Japanese and Korean speakers in apologies and requests? Is the amount of information influenced by different situations in Japanese and Korean? What information is preferred in Japanese and Korean, respectively?
(3) Are the sentence types of utterances that help convey the speaker's intention clearly different in Japanese and Korean? What sentences types are used frequently in comparable situations in Japanese and Korean?
(4) Is the responsibility for the understanding of utterances influenced by the speaker's social features such as age, gender, occupation, residence, or the relationship between the speaker and the listener?

2.8　Hypothesis

The hypothesis of the present research is that Japanese tends to be a listener-responsible language and Korean is disposed to be a speaker-responsible language on the level of conversation. In order to demonstrate the hypothesis, the amount of information and the types of sentences uttered by research participants will be analyzed. The more information uttered, the more helpful it is for the listener to understand utterances. If the sentence types match the purpose of the conversation, it helps the listener more easily understand the utterances.

The methods will be described in the next chapter.

Endnotes

1 Therefore, the present research does not suggest a universal theory that includes other languages such as American English, Chinese, etc.
2 The terms EFL and ESL are used differently in accordance with the previous studies cited in the present study. The term EFL (not ESL) is used when the author introduces Qi & Liu (2007) because the term EFL was used by them in their paper.
3 Hall (1976) pointed out that Japanese is a language of high-context culture and English is a language of low-context culture.
4 Ogiwara (2008) was cited from Horie & Pardeshi (2009) in the present study. I translated the original Japanese into English.
5 Horie & Pardeshi (2009) wrote the paper in Japanese and I translated it into English.
6 The reason why the speech acts apologies and requests were selected will be described in Chapter 3 more in detail.
7 The Japanese word 'Shiage' which was translated into English as 'Finishing' is on of the features of Japanese conversation. "Yoroshiku onegaishimasu" is an example of finishing.

Chapter 3

Methodology

3.1   General Account

In this chapter, the methodology of the present research is described. Based on the research findings of the pilot study discussed in Chapter 2, the total amount of utterances and types of utterances are focused on in order to support the hypothesis of this study, namely: Japanese is a listener-responsible language and Korean is a speaker-responsible language. If the speaker utters detailed information and uses sentence types which match the speaker's real intention, it means that the speaker takes responsibility for the understanding of the utterance.

3.2   Experimental Design of Conversation Situations

In the pilot study (Yoon, 2009), real conversations by Japanese and Korean married couples were recorded and analyzed. However, the number of participants was limited to nine Japanese and ten Korean married couples. Thus, a descriptive questionnaire and a DCT (Discourse Completion Test) were conducted after setting up two corresponding situations, apologies and requests, which were completed by the Japanese and Korean couples. The merits of the questionnaire and DCT are that it is possible to gather a large amount of data and to compare different languages objectively.

The DCT was conducted in the classroom for JU and KU, while JIU and KIU completed the DCT individually outside the classroom. The DCT was originally developed to compare the speech act realizations of native and nonnative

Hebrew speakers (Blum-Kulka, 1982, following Levenston, 1975). The test consists of scripted dialogues which are preceded by a short description of the situation specifying the setting and the social distance between the participants and their status relative to each other (Blum-Kulka *et al.*, 1989). The DCT used for the present study was made by the author in light of Blum-Kulka *et al.* (1989) to compare the ways in which Japanese and Korean speakers use apology expressions. The descriptive questionnaire was conducted by office workers individually in both Japanese and Korean[1].

The DCT and the descriptive questionnaire were set up to examine not only the differences in responsibility for understanding utterances, but also cross-cultural variations in the two speech acts apologies and requests between Japanese and Korean speakers.

There are two reasons why apologies and requests were analyzed to investigate the responsibility for understanding utterances. First, as described in the previous chapter, apologies and requests are both *face-threatening acts* (Brown and Levinson, 1987), and both speech acts are costly to the listener (Blum-Kulka *et al.*, 1989), thus, the speaker should utter something more than the two speech acts in quotation to their interlocutors. Furthermore, there is a difference between the speech acts: Apology is a speech act in which the speaker conveys their emotion about how they negatively affected the listener, while request is a speech act in which the speaker should make their interlocutor do something for them.

Second, apologies and requests are both very important for inter-cultural communication (Blum-Kulka *et al.*, 1989). The results of this study can find applications in the field of inter-cultural communication between Japanese and Korean speakers. Thus, to confirm and understand the differences between the two languages is very meaningful and instructive for smooth inter-cultural communication.

Blum-Kulka *et al.* (1989) also introduced the two speech acts by quoting Leech (1980) as post-event (apologies) and pre-event (requests) as follows:

> Both speech acts apologies and requests concern events that are costly to the listener[2]. However, the request, in requiring a future effort from the interlocutor, imposes mainly on the listener, while the apology, as an attempt by the speaker to make up for some pervious action that interfered with the listener's interests, counteracts the speaker's face wants.
>
> (Blum-Kulka *et al.*, 1989: 12)

3.3 Participants

In this section specific information about the participants, methods, and data analysis is also described.

Survey participants were divided into two groups: the first group was made up of Japanese university students and office workers and the second group was made up of Korean university students and office workers. The university students were divided into two sub groups: Japanese and Korean university students in their native countries, and Japanese and Korean university students in the United States of America[3]. The utterances of both university students and office workers were analyzed because it was assumed that more accurate and objective results can be found by using various data collection methods and by analyzing utterances of various groups of informants. Except for the university students living in the U.S., all Japanese participants were living in the capital sphere of Tokyo and all Korean participants were living in the capital sphere of Seoul at the time of this survey. In addition, none of the participants studied Korean or Japanese as a foreign language before the research was completed. Specific information on each of the participant groups is described in the next section.

3.3.1 University Students

Table 3-1 represents the information of Japanese and Korean university students.

Table 3-1. Participants (university students) information

	Number (people)	Age (years)	Length of stay in the U.S. (months)
JU (M/F)	101 (55 / 46)	18.7 (18.3 / 18.6)	
KU(M/F)	71 (29 / 42)[4]	19.5 (20.8 / 19.4)	
JIU(M/F)	34 (18 / 16)	24.5 (23.9 / 25.1)	37.8 (41.3 / 34.3)
KIU(M/F)	58 (32 / 26)	26.3 (28.2 / 24.4)	33.9 (36.8 / 31.0)

JU: Japanese university students who live in Japan
KU: Korean university students who live in Korea
JIU: Japanese international university students who live in the U.S.
KIU: Korean international university students who live in the U.S.
M: Male students
F: Female students

3.3.1.1 Japanese and Korean University Students Who Live in Their Own Countries

101 (male: 55, female: 46) Japanese (Mean age = 18.7 years; Range = 18–24 years old) and 71 (male: 29, female: 42) Korean (Mean age = 19.5 years; Range = 18–24 years old) university students made up this group. Korean participants were requested to write how old they would be in Japan on the survey sheet because the way of calculating age is different in Japan and Korea. Also, in Korea, a male is enrolled in the military for about two years after he turns 18 years old, and many male university students enter military service after finishing their freshmen year. All the male Korean university participants of this group had not joined the military service yet to control for age variances. Being in the military for about two years may influence Korean males' verbal communication.

3.3.1.2 Japanese and Korean University Students Who Live in the United States of America

34 (male: 18, female: 16) Japanese (Mean age = 24.5 years; Range = 19–32 years old) and 58 (male: 32, female: 26) Korean (Mean age = 26.3 years; Range = 20–35 years old) university students who were studying at the time of this study at universities which are located in Washington, D.C. and Boston, Massachusetts in the United States of America made up this group. The Japanese students' average length of stay in the United States of America was 37.8 months (Range = 6–120 months) and the Koreans' was 33.9 months (Range = 6–84 months). Korean participants who lived in the U.S. included males who were discharged from military duty.

3.3.2 Office Workers

The office workers were made up of Japanese and Korean company employees, living in the capital spheres of Tokyo and Seoul, respectively, in their 20's and 30's, and college educated. Specifically, 42 (20 males Mean age = 27.9 years, 22 females Mean age = 27.8 years) Japanese (Mean age = 27.9 years; Range = 23–39 years old) and 40 (15 males Mean age = 31.1 years, 25 females Mean age = 28.9 years) Korean (Mean age = 29.8 years; Range = 23–37 years old) office workers made up this group.

3.4 Methods

In order to compare the responsibility for understanding utterances in Japanese and Korean objectively, different methods were employed for each participant group.

3.4.1 University Students

A DCT (Discourse Completion Test) was completed by Japanese and Korean university students to compare differences with respect to speaker responsibility. Using the DCT can show not only the total amount of information, but also when speakers convey their real intentions in the conversation. The DCT, which is used in the present research and has been translated from Japanese and Korean into English, is shown below.

3.4.1.1 Apologies

You arranged to meet your good friend in front of a movie theatre to see a movie. But you are about 20 minutes late.

> You: (   )
> Friend: "That's OK. It couldn't be helped because your class finished late."
> You: (   )
> Friend: "Ticket? I have already bought two tickets."
> You: (   )
> Friend: "You don't have to thank me for just the movie ticket."

3.4.1.2 Requests

You are visiting a professor to submit your term paper. However, the professor is saying that your term paper will not be accepted because the deadline has passed already.

> Professor: "The deadline was the day before yesterday."
> You: (   )
> Professor: "No, you don't have to apologize."
> You: (   )
> Professor: "If I accept your term paper, it would be unfair to the other students."

3.4.2 Office Workers

For the purpose of this research, descriptive questionnaires were conducted to compare the amount of information in Japanese and Korean conversations, and how their differences can be relevant in terms of the interpretation of the speaker's intention. The questionnaire, which is used in this research and has been translated from Japanese and Korean into English, is shown below.

3.4.2.1 Apologies
You are about 10 minutes late for a business meeting. What do you say to the following people?

Boss: (	)
Colleague: (	)
Subordinate: (	)

3.4.2.2 Requests
You have not eaten lunch yet because you are very busy now. You want to ask a person from your office, who is going to convenience store, to get you a sandwich. What do you say to the following people?

Boss: (	)
Colleague: (	)
Subordinate: (	)

3.5 Data Analysis

Two types of analyses were conducted, one statistical and one qualitative. The importance of integrating quantitative and qualitative analyses are discussed in the section on methodological concerns below.

3.5.1 Quantitative Analysis
ANOVAs were used to reveal the differences in the amount of information found in corresponding situations in Japanese and Korean. Also, the types of sentences uttered were analyzed statistically.

It is not adequate to simply calculate the number words or sentences to compare information in utterances in Japanese and Korean, because there is not a one-to-one correspondence of linguistic items between both languages. Therefore, the data obtained from the participants was analyzed quantitatively using semantic formulas[5] i.e., the various verbal realizations of an apology and a request, with respect to information uttered by Japanese and Korean speakers in corresponding situations (Beebe, Takahashi, & Uliss-Weltz, 1990; Tao, 2007).

Semantic formulas are types of semantic units in a speech act, all the utterances involved in completing the dialogue in the DCT were analyzed and identified as semantic formulas for the purpose of this study. For example:

<u>Hey mate,</u>   I am <u>really</u> <u>sorry</u> <u>I am late.</u> <u>The lecture finished late</u>[6].
(Address term)   (Adverb)   (Fact)   (Reason)
                    (Apology)

The analysis of semantic formulas can clarify not only the amount of information in the utterances but also construction patterns of the utterances in apologies by Japanese and Korean speakers. The semantic formulas are different depending on the participant group and the situation. Specific semantic formulas will be described in the chapter when necessary.

3.5.2 Qualitative Analysis

In addition to statistical analyses, a qualitative analysis of several issues, such as the analysis of the pattern of using stereotyped utterances of semantic formulas in Japanese and Korean was conducted.

In the next chapter, apology discourse by Japanese and Korean university students will be discussed.

Endnotes

1 The present study focuses on the differences of responsibility for understanding utterances between Japanese and Korean but not between university students and office workers in Japanese or Korean. Therefore, different surveys were conducted for university students and office workers.
2 Blum-Kulka *et al*. (1989) used the term *hearer* instead of *listener* but listener was replaced by the author in the present study to prevent confusion.
3 The present study basically focused on the difference of the responsibility for understanding utterances between Japanese and Korean people who live their own countries. The international Japanese and Korean university students who live in the U.S. were surveyed to examine whether daily use of English, which is a speaker-responsible language, can influence conversations in their native languages or not.

4 The number of Korean female university students is more than that of Korean male university students. However, female and male participants were analyzed separately, and the statistical analysis took those differences into account.
5 The units of language that have meaning.
6 An example translated into English from real conversational data which the author gathered from Japanese and Korean participants.

Chapter 4

Apology Discourse by Japanese and Korean University Students

4.1 General Account

The purpose of this chapter is to show that Japanese is a listener-responsible language, while Korean is a speaker-responsible language on the level of conversational communication by comparing conversations by Japanese and Korean university students making apologies. The informants in the present chapter consisted of four groups: Japanese university students who live in their own country, Japanese university students who live in the U.S.; Korean university students who live in their own country and Korean university students who live in the United States of America. A Discourse Completion Test (DCT) was completed by Japanese and Korean university students to compare the cultural differences of speaker responsibility in apologies. The results suggest that Korean should be classified as a speaker-responsible language for understanding in conversations, since Korean speakers produce much more information and convey more information per utterance to the interlocutor than Japanese speakers. Furthermore, it is found that the responsibility for understanding utterances positively correlates with daily use of American English, especially in the case of Japanese university students.

4.2 Introduction

In this chapter, the differences in responsibility for understanding utterances in Japanese and Korean in apologies are examined by comparing conversations by

Japanese and Korean university students, in order to clarify that Japanese is a listener-responsible language and Korean is a speaker-responsible language on the conversation level, even though both are currently categorized as listener-responsible languages (Hinds, 1987). Also, whether or not acquisition or daily use of English, which is categorized as a speaker-responsible language by Hinds (1987), influences the speaking patterns of Japanese and Korean speakers in terms of responsibility for understanding utterances is examined by analyzing the utterances spoken by Japanese university students and Korean university students who live in the United States of America. Three research questions arise in this chapter:

(1) Japanese and Korean are different in the total amount of information embedded in utterances per turn. Which language has a higher amount of information embedded per turn?

(2) Which semantic formulas are preferred for appropriate communication in apology discourse in Japanese and Korean, respectively?

(3) Does the daily use of English influence the use of native Japanese and Korean with respect to the responsibility for understanding utterances?

4.3 Data Analysis

The DCT (Discourse Completion Test), which is used in this chapter and has been translated from Japanese and Korean into English, is shown below.

You arranged to meet a good friend in front of a movie theater to see a movie, but you are about 20 minutes late.

| You: (   ) |
| Friend: "That's OK. It couldn't be helped because your class finished late." |
| You: (   ) |
| Friend: "Ticket? I have already bought two tickets." |
| You: (   ) |
| Friend: "You don't have to thank me for just the movie ticket." |

Table 4-1, 4-2, and 4-3 below show which semantic formulas were used in utterances in the first, the second, and the third turn, respectively. The ADVERB and the INTERJECTION occur before or after the APOLOGY or THANKS expressions in the first and second turn. It is well known that Japanese speakers usually use an apology expression like "sumimasen" or "gomen" as a thankful expression (Kim, 1996; Ide, 1998; Jin, 2004; Yamamoto, 2003) and sometimes in Korean an apology expression like "mianhay" is also used in appreciations. It is hard to decide whether "gomen" and "mianhay" are used for apology or appreciation in the DCT. Even though the situation set for the DCT in the present study is an apology for being late for an appointment fundamentally, the participants might say "Thank you" for understanding the reasons for being late or getting a ticket from their friends. Thus, the apology expressions "gomen" or "mianhay" are categorized literally as semantic formula APOLOGY and the thankful expressions "arigato" or "komawe" are categorized as semantic formula THANKS in the second and the third turn.

Utterances about buying movie tickets, for example, "Let's go buy tickets" or "Have you bought the tickets yet?" are regarded as the semantic formula TICKET in the second turn. And utterances about worrying that the movie has already started are regarded as the semantic formula MOVIE in the second turn.

Table 4-1. Semantic formulas and examples in the first turn in university students' apologies

	Semantic formulas	Examples
1	APOLOGY	"I am sorry."
2	FACT	"I am late."
3	REASON	"The lecture finished late."
4	ADVERB	"(I am) really (sorry)."
5	ADDRESS TERM	"John!"
6	INTERJECTION	"Oh, (sorry)."
7	OTHERS	"When did you get here?"

Table 4-2. Semantic formulas and examples in the second turn

	Semantic formulas	Examples
1	APOLOGY	"I am sorry."
2	THANKS	"Thank you."
3	TICKET	"Let's go buy tickets."
4	MOVIE	"Do you think the movie's started already?"
5	COMPENSATION	"I will buy you some popcorn."
6	OTHERS	"I don't like the professor."

Table 4-3. Semantic formulas and examples in the third turn

	Semantic formulas	Examples
1	APOLOGY	"I am sorry."
2	THANKS	"Thank you."
3	SURPRISE	"Really?"
4	COMPLIMENT	"You are a good friend."
5	COMPENSATION	"I will buy you some popcorn!"
6	INTERJECTION	"Oh, (thanks)."
7	ADVERB	"(I) Really (appreciate it)."
8	OTHERS	"You shouldn't have bought the ticket for me."

4.4　Results

4.4.1　The First Turn of Apologetic Discourse

(1) Comparison Between Japanese and Korean University Students

Table 4-4 indicates the total amount of information that was used in the first turn for JU and KU. The ANOVA revealed that the amount of information used in Korean utterances was significantly higher than Japanese utterances with respect to the semantic formulas REASON, ADDRESS TERM, and INTERJECTION. As for the semantic formula ADVERB, a significant difference was found between KMU and JMU: KMU used ADVERB significantly more than JMU. Also, there was a significant difference between female and male Japanese students regarding ADVERB: JFU uttered the semantic formula ADVERB significantly more than JMU.

Table 4-4. Total amount of information in the first turn of JU and KU in apologies

		Female	Male	χ^2 ANOVA (two way) by arcsin asin	χ^2		Post hoc analysis
1	JU	100.0	94.5	Nationality	1.63		
	KU	95.2	96.6	Gender	2.29		
				Interaction	4.19		
2	JU	54.3	50.9	Nationality	0.78		
	KU	45.2	48.3	Gender	0.00		
				Interaction	0.24		
3	JU	43.5	58.2	Nationality	11.20	*	KU>JU
	KU	78.6	65.5	Gender	0.00		
				Interaction	4.91		
4	JU	19.6	3.6	Nationality	6.64	*	KMU>JMU
	KU	28.6	17.2	Gender	9.25	*	JFU>JMU
				Interaction	0.97		
5	JU	0.0	0.0	Nationality	36.92	*	KU>JU
	KU	21.4	10.3	Gender	1.35		
				Interaction	1.35		
6	JU	0.0	1.8	Nationality	55.85	*	KU>JU
	KU	26.2	31.0	Gender	1.99		
				Interaction	0.38		
7	JU	0.0	1.8	Nationality	5.82	*	KFU>JFU
	KU	7.1	3.4	Gender	0.14		
				Interaction	2.71		

Note: *p<0.05, Unit: %, 1: Apology, 2: Fact, 3: Reason, 4: Adverb, 5: Address Term, 6: Interjection, 7: Others, JU: Japanese university students, KU: Korean university students, JMU: Japanese male university students, JFU: Japanese female university students, KMU: Korean male university students, KFU: Korean female university students.

(2) Influence of Daily Use of English

Table 4-5 shows the total amount of information in the first turn of JU, KU, JIU, and KIU.

Table 4-5. Total amount of information in the first turn of JU, KU, JIU, and KIU in apologies

		JU	KU		χ^2 ANOVA (two way) by arcsin asin		Post hoc analysis
					χ^2		
1	JU/KU	97.0	95.8	English	0.03		
	JIU/KIU	97.1	94.7	Nationality	0.48		
				Interaction	0.05		
2	JU/KU	52.5	46.5	English	7.68	*	JU/JIU: JIU>JU
	JIU/KIU	76.5	57.9	Nationality	3.83		
				Interaction	1.13		
3	JU/KU	51.5	73.2	English	12.20	*	KU/KIU: KU>KIU
	JIU/KIU	50.0	29.8	Nationality	0.02		
				Interaction	10.67	*	JU/KU: KU>JU, JIU/KIU: JIU>KIU
4	JU/KU	10.9	23.9	English	2.70		
	JIU/KIU	5.9	14.0	Nationality	5.53	*	JU/KU: KU>JU
				Interaction	0.07		
5	JU/KU	0.0	16.9	English	0.01		
	JIU/KIU	2.9	7.0	Nationality	15.32	*	JU/KU: KU>JU
				Interaction	6.05	*	JU/JIU: JIU>JU, KU/KIU: KU>KIU
6	JU/KU	1.0	28.1	English	5.08	*	KU/KIU: KU>KIU
	JIU/KIU	2.9	3.5	Nationality	12.80	*	JU/KU: KU>JU
				Interaction	11.03	*	
7	JU/KU	1.0	4.2	English	13.91	*	JIU/KIU > JU/KU
	JIU/KIU	14.7	15.8	Nationality	0.84		
				Interaction	0.47		

Note: *p<0.05, Unit: %, 1: Apology, 2: Fact, 3: Reason, 4: Adverb, 5: Address Term, 6: Interjection, 7: Others, JU: Japanese university students, KU: Korean university students, JIU: Japanese international university students who live in the U.S., KIU: Korean international university students who live in the U.S.

Significant differences were found for the semantic formulas FACT, REASON, and INTERJECTION because of the main effect of using English in daily conversation. The mention rate of FACT by JIU was significantly higher than JU's. KU uttered REASON and INTERJECTION significantly more than KIU.

4.4.2 The Second Turn of Apologetic Discourse
(1) Comparison between Japanese and Korean University Students

Table 4-6 shows the total amount of information by JU and KU in the second turn. Regarding nationality, the ANOVA revealed significant differences for all semantic formulas in the second turn except OTHERS between Japanese and Korean. KMU uttered APOLOGY significantly more than JMU. KFU uttered THANKS significantly more than JFU. JU uttered TICKET significantly more than KU. KU uttered MOVIE and COMPENSATION significantly more than JU.

There were three significant differences in regards to gender in the second turn. First, both JFU and KFU uttered the semantic formula TICKET significantly more than JMU and KMU, respectively. Second, JFU uttered APOLOGY significantly more than JMU. Finally, KMU uttered THANKS significantly more than KFU.

Table 4-6. Total amount of information in the second turn of JU and KU in apologies

		Female	Male		χ^2 ANOVA (two way) by arcsin asin χ^2		Post hoc analysis
1	JU	35.6	9.1	Nationality	0.23		
	KU	26.2	20.7	Gender	8.96	*	JU: JFU>JMU
				Interaction	4.06	*	MU: KU>JU
2	JU	11.1	12.7	Nationality	10.87	*	FU: JU>KU
	KU	0.0	6.9	Gender	4.78	*	KU: KMU>KFU
				Interaction	3.29		
3	JU	97.8	87.3	Nationality	7.02	*	JU>KU
	KU	88.1	75.9	Gender	8.02	*	FU>MU
				Interaction	0.17		
4	JU	2.2	1.8	Nationality	22.79	*	KU>JU
	KU	26.2	13.8	Gender	1.66		
				Interaction	1.15		
5	JU	0.0	0.0	Nationality	42.39	*	KU>JU
	KU	11.9	24.1	Gender	1.47		
				Interaction	1.47		
6	JU	2.2	1.8	Nationality	1.08		
	KU	2.4	6.9	Gender	0.52		
				Interaction	0.88		

Note: *p<0.05, Unit: %, 1: Apology, 2: Thanks, 3: Ticket, 4: Movie, 5: Compensation, 6: Others, JU: Japanese university students, KU: Korean university students, JMU: Japanese male university students, JFU: Japanese female university students, KMU: Korean male university students, KFU: Korean female university students, FU: female university students, MU: male university students.

(2) Influence of Daily Use of English

Table 4-7 shows the results of the ANOVA for the total amount of information in the second turn. JIU uttered the semantic formula APOLOGY significantly more than JU, while KU uttered APOLOGY significantly more than KIU. JIU uttered the semantic formula COMPENSATION significantly more than JU.

Table 4-7. Total amount of information in the second turn of JU, KU, JIU, and KIU in apologies

		JU	KU		χ^2 ANOVA (two way) by arcsin asin		Post hoc analysis
					χ^2		
1	JU/KU	21.0	23.9	English	0.00		
	JIU/KIU	38.2	10.3	Nationality	5.26	*	JIU/KIU: JIU>KIU
				Interaction	7.93	*	JU/JIU:JIU>JU, KU/KIU:KU>KIU
2	JU/KU	12.0	2.8	English	0.07		
	JIU/KIU	8.8	3.4	Nationality	5.14	*	JU/KU: JU>KU
				Interaction	0.28		
3	JU/KU	92.0	83.1	English	3.14		
	JIU/KIU	82.4	75.9	Nationality	2.67		
				Interaction	0.18		
4	JU/KU	2.0	21.1	English	0.16		
	JIU/KIU	5.9	17.2	Nationality	15.17	*	KU/KIU>JU>JIU
				Interaction	1.33		
5	JU/KU	0.0	16.9	English	5.61	*	JU/JIU: JIU>JU
	JIU/KIU	5.9	22.4	Nationality	25.51	*	KU/KIU>JU/JIU
				Interaction	1.75		
6	JU/KU	2.0	4.2	English	9.38	*	JIU/KIU>JU/KU
	JIU/KIU	11.8	15.5	Nationality	0.79		
				Interaction	0.01		

Note: *p<0.05, Unit: %, 1: Apology, 2: Thanks, 3: Ticket, 4: Movie, 5: Compensation, 6: Others, JU: Japanese university students, KU: Korean university students, JIU: Japanese international university students who live in the U.S., KIU: Korean international university students who live in the U.S.

4.4.3 The Third Turn of Apologetic Discourse
(1) Comparison between Japanese and Korean University Students
Table 4-8 shows the total amount of information in the third turn of JU and KU in apologies. An ANOVA was conducted in order to determine whether the speakers' mention rates of semantic formulas were different depending on the speaker's nationality or gender. The ANOVA revealed that KU's mention rates of

semantic formulas were significantly higher than JU's for two semantic formulas: COMPENSATION and INTERJECTION. And it was revealed that KMU uttered APOLOGY significantly more than JMU. The ANOVA also revealed that JU's mention rate of APOLOGY was significantly higher than KU's.

(2) Influence of Daily Use of English
Table 4-9 shows the total amount of information in the third turn of JU, KU, JIU, and KIU in apologies.

As Table 4-9 shows, there were four significant differences between JU/KU and JIU/KIU. As for the semantic formulas THANKS and INTERJECTION, KU's mention rates were significantly higher than KIU's. However, JIU's mention rate of the semantic formula INTERJECTION was higher than JU's. For semantic formula COMPLIMENT, JU's mention rate was significantly higher than JIU's.

4.5 Discussion

4.5.1 Explanations for Apology Preferred by Korean Students

As shown clearly in the results for the mention rates of the semantic formulas above, Korean speakers tend to explain their situation positively, while Japanese speakers leave the understanding of the situation to the interlocutors. As for the semantic formula REASON in the first turn, Korean students tried to explain the reasons why they were late for the appointment to the listeners actively. In contrast, only about 50% of Japanese students referred to the reasons despite having a particular reason that the lecture finished late in the DCT.

Surprisingly, little attention has been given to the strategy of apology in the field of comparison study between Japanese and Korean, since it is easy to assume that there are few differences because of cultural, linguistic, and geographic similarity. Most of the studies that are associated with apology have focused mainly on the expressions of apology in Japanese and Korean (Ogoshi, 1993; Kim, 1996; Jin, 2004; Hong, 2006).

However, there are some contrastive studies of apology strategies between Japanese and American speakers. Kondo & Taniguchi (2007) compared the apology strategies between Japanese and American English speakers and found that the impressions of giving reasons for their apology are different. Japanese listeners take the reason as a 'defense', while American speakers, who speak English

Table 4-8. Total amount of information in the third turn of JU and KU in apologies

		Female	Male		χ^2 ANOVA (two way) by arcsin asin χ^2		Post hoc analysis
1	JU	21.7	7.3	Nationality	5.25	*	KMU>JMU
	KU	31.0	20.7	Gender	6.13	*	JFU>JMU
				Interaction	0.49		
2	JU			Nationality	18.02	*	JU>KU
	KU	71.4	75.9	Gender	1.53		
				Interaction	4.02		
3	JU	43.5	32.7	Nationality	3.20		
	KU	54.8	44.8	Gender	2.54		
				Interaction	0.01		
4	JU	6.5	20.0	Nationality	1.67		
	KU	16.7	20.7	Gender	3.74		
				Interaction	1.35		
5	JU	0.0	0.0	Nationality	54.36	*	KU>JU
	KU	42.9	6.9	Gender	11.38	*	KFU>KMU
				Interaction	11.38	*	
6	JU	10.9	7.3	Nationality	124.17	*	KU>JU
	KU	73.8	75.9	Gender	0.08		
				Interaction	0.43		
7	JU	21.7	9.1	Nationality	2.92		
	KU	31.0	17.2	Gender	6.58	*	JFU/KFU>JMU/KMU
				Interaction	0.01		
8	JU	6.5	9.1	Nationality	21.46	*	KU>JU
	KU	21.4	41.4	Gender	4.03	*	KMU>KFU
				Interaction	1.62		

Note: *p<0.05, Unit: %, 1: Apology, 2: Thanks, 3: Surprise, 4: Compliment, 5: Compensation, 6: Interjection, 7: Adverb, 8: Others, JU: Japanese university students, KU: Korean university students, JMU: Japanese male university students, JFU: Japanese female university students, KMU: Korean male university students, KFU: Korean female university students.

Table 4–9. Total amount of information in the third turn of JU, KU, JIU, and KIU in apologies

		J	K		χ^2 ANOVA (two way) by arcsin asin		Post hoc analysis
					χ^2		
1	JU/KU	13.9	26.8	English	2.21		
	JIU/KIU	8.8	17.2	Nationality	4.71	*	JU/KU: KU>JU
				Interaction	0.07		
2	JU/KU	92.1	73.2	English	4.22	*	KU/KIU: KU>KIU
	JIU/KIU	88.2	53.4	Nationality	24.65	*	JU/JIU>KU/KIU
				Interaction	1.13		
3	JU/KU	37.6	50.7	English	0.92		
	JIU/KIU	41.2	34.5	Nationality	0.23		
				Interaction	2.30		
4	JU/KU	13.9	18.3	English	5.02	*	JU/JIU: JU>JIU
	JIU/KIU	2.9	12.1	Nationality	3.37		
				Interaction	0.87		
5	JU/KU	0.0	28.2	English	13.00	*	JU/JIU: JIU>JU
	JIU/KIU	14.7	36.2	Nationality	37.32	*	JIU/KIU>JU/KU
				Interaction	5.36	*	
6	JU/KU	8.9	74.6	English	0.84		
	JIU/KIU	50.0	39.7	Nationality	22.89	*	JU/KU: KU>JU
				Interaction	40.26	*	JU/JIU:JIU>JU, KU/KIU:KU>KIU
7	JU/KU	14.9	25.4	English	2.17		
	JIU/KIU	8.8	17.2	Nationality	3.78		
				Interaction	0.00		
8	JU/KU	7.9	29.6	English	0.01		
	JIU/KIU	14.7	19.0	Nationality	6.85	*	JU/KU: KU>JU
				Interaction	3.07		

Note: *$p<0.05$, Unit: %, 1: Apology, 2: Thanks, 3: Surprise, 4: Compliment, 5: Compensation, 6: Interjection, 7: Adverb, 8: Others, JU: Japanese university students, KU: Korean university students, JIU: Japanese international university students who live in the U.S., KIU: Korean international university students who live in the U.S.

as a speaker-responsible language according to Hinds (1987), regard it as a 'polite explanation' in apologies. In her comparison of strategies of apology between Japanese and Americans, Ikeda (1993) also described that American speakers use the explanation strategy more than Japanese. The results of Ikeda (1993) are similar to those of the present study. Ikeda (1993) also pointed out that Japanese speakers tend to utter only apology expressions without any other strategic utterances, while American speakers utter not only explanation but also compensation expressions with apologies. The ANOVA revealed that Korean speakers utter compensation expressions significantly more than Japanese speakers in the present study. In the third turn, Japanese students uttered only expressions of apology or appreciation, while Korean students added compensation when they knew that their friends had bought two tickets already, as shown:

Friend: "Tickets? I have bought two tickets already."
Japanese: "Arigato."
    (Thank you)
Korean: "Komawe. Nayka phapkhon salkey."
    (Thank you. Let me buy some popcorn.)

Korean speakers used the semantic formula COMPENSATION in the second turn to compensate their friends for being late by offering to buy their friends a ticket, while no Japanese speakers uttered COMPENSATION and they only suggested to their friends that they should buy tickets together, or asked whether the friends had bought the tickets already or not, as shown in the conversation below.

Friend: "That's OK. It couldn't be helped because the class finished late."
Japanese: "Gomen. Tokorode chikettowa mo katta?"
    (I am sorry. By the way did you buy your ticket already?)
Korean: "Mian. Kutaysin thikheysun nayka salkey."
    (I am sorry. I will buy a ticket for you then.)

According to Ikeda (1993), the difference between Japanese and American speakers is caused by the difference in attitudes to *face* (Brown & Levinson, 1987) in both countries. In other words, the *face* to Japanese speakers is deeply related to being admitted and accepted by their interlocutors because of the vertical social-cultural structure (*tate shakai*) in Japan. It is for that reason that Japanese speakers tend to avoid using the explanation strategy, especially when they talk to a person who is older or of higher status than themselves, and they try to put weight on conveying an apology expression itself and apologize efficiently.

Japanese and Korean social structures are fairly similar compared to that of the U.S., thus it is hard to explain the phenomena by just the difference of social structures, since the tendency of Korean speakers to give a reason for their apology in the results of the current paper is similar to that of American speakers. It is suggested that Korean is a speaker-responsible language similar to American English, since Korean and American English share some features with respect to giving extra explanations to help listeners' understanding of utterances, even though Korean was categorized as a listener-responsible language by Hinds (1987).

In terms of speech act, it can also be pointed out that the apology is conceptualized differently in Japanese and Korean. In other words, Japanese speakers accept just saying the apologetic expression "Sumimasen" as an apology, whereas Korean speakers consider uttering not only apologetic expression but also the reason, compensation, etc. as an apology.

There was no significant difference between Japanese and Korean for the utterance rate of the semantic formula COMPLIMENT in the third turn. However, it was found that the ways of uttering COMPLIMENT were different in Japanese and Korean. Korean speakers tend to utter a complete sentence in order to comment about and convey their thankful emotion for receiving a movie ticket, while Japanese speakers tend to use only a typical word for compliment like "sasuga" (just as one thought) or "yahari" (as expected) as the example below:

Friend: "Tickets? I have bought two tickets already."
Japanese: "Arigato. Sasuga."
    (Thank you. It's just (like you to buy a ticket already)).
Korean: "Komawe. Yeksi netapta."
    (Thank you. It's just like you (buy a ticket already)).

4.5.2 Expressions of Apology and Thanks
Even though the situation set by the researcher in the present chapter was basically an apology, many Japanese and Korean participants mixed apologetic expressions and thankful expressions in use, especially in the second and the third

turns. Two reasons could account for this. First, the participants who were late reacted differently when their friend arrived on time and bought them a ticket. Some participants felt sorry and some participants felt appreciation in the same situation. Second, it is hard to distinguish between the two expressions for apology and thanks clearly in Japanese and Korean compared to the English "I am sorry" and "Thank you." It is well known that the Japanese expression for apology "sumimasen" is also used as an expression of appreciation in Japanese discourse, as described above (Kim, 1996; Ide, 1998; Yamamoto, 2003). For example, on someone's birthday the following kind of conversations could happen in both Japan and Korea, but not in the U.S:

A: "Happy birthday! Here you are. I hope you like this present."
B: "I am sorry."
 (Japanese: Sumimasen.)
 (Korean: Mianhakey…)

In the example of receiving a birthday present above, a Korean speaker might not say as conclusively "I am sorry" as a Japanese speaker, that is why little attention has been paid to the use of Korean apology expressions as thankful expressions in past research. It is interesting that Korean speakers say "Mianhakey" which means "I feel sorry I made you to do this for me" while they don't use "I am sorry" in situations showing appreciation.

The results of the third turn in the present chapter show that Korean male speakers uttered apologetic expressions when they found that their friend had bought a movie ticket for them significantly more than Japanese male speakers. Korean female speakers uttered apologetic expressions more than Japanese female speakers even though there was no significant difference between them (about 9.3 points). Also, Korean male speakers uttered apologetic expressions significantly more than Japanese male speakers in the second turn when their friend said he or she could understand why they had been late for the appointment. It is reasonable to suppose that Korean speakers try to convey the emotion that they feel sorry for being late for the appointment to the interlocutor actively by uttering apologetic expressions through all the turns. Also, the results of the present chapter are different from those of Kim (1996) which claimed that Korean speakers barely use apologetic expressions in thanks. Thus, it will be necessary to examine what kinds of expressions are used for apology and thanks in Japanese and Korean in other situations.

Korean speakers also used the semantic formulas ADVERB and INTERJECTION, which modify the apologetic and thankful expressions, in order to convey their feeling actively. It has been pointed out that both Japanese and Korean speakers use adverbs more in apologetic expressions than thankful ones if the feelings of apology are stronger or the interlocutor is older than the speakers (Kim, 1996). The results clearly show that Korean speakers use more of the semantic formulas ADVERB and INTERJECTION right before or after expressions of apology or thanks compared to Japanese speakers in corresponding situations.

It was found that Korean speakers used the semantic formula ADDRESS TERM in the first turn while no Japanese speakers used the semantic formula ADDRESS TERM. The results confirm the claim of Yoon (2008) that Korean speakers use address terms as *contextualization cues* (Gumperz, 1982) more frequently in conversations compared to Japanese speakers. In the present research, many Korean speakers uttered "Chinguya" which means "Hey, friend" in order to attract the listener's interest and to make sure that the relationship between the speaker and the listener (good friends) is established and stays unchanged before or after saying "I am sorry."

4.5.3 Influence of Daily Use of English in Responsibility for Understanding Utterances

In regards to whether daily use of English, which is classified as a speaker-responsible language, can influence the ways Japanese and Korean speakers use their native languages, the results show that JIU used more semantic formulas than JU generally. The ANOVA revealed that JIU uttered the semantic formulas FACT and ADDRESS TERM in the first turn, APOLOGY and COMPENSATION in the second turn, and COMPENSATION and INTERJECTION in the third turn significantly more than JU. It is interesting that JIU uttered FACT significantly more than JU in apologies and FACT was the only semantic formula that JIU and KIU uttered more than JU and KU, respectively, though there is no significant difference between KU and KIU. Regarding semantic formulas ADDRESS TERM in the first turn and COMPENSATION in the second turn, nobody in JU uttered either semantic formula. The data suggests that Japanese, which is classified as a listener-responsible language, could be influenced by English, which is regarded as a speaker-responsible language.

KIU's total amount of information is significantly lower than KU's with respect to the semantic formulas REASON, ADDRESS TERM, and INTERJECTION in the first turn, APOLOGY in the second turn, and THANKS and INTERJECTION in the third turn.

4.6　Conclusions

The present chapter set out to investigate the differences between Japanese and Korean speakers' responsibility for the understanding of utterances in a conversation. The experiment was carried out to compare how semantic formulas are used in utterances as helpful information for the listeners in corresponding situations in both Japanese and Korean. To the first research question, the results of the current chapter suggest that Korean should be classified as a speaker-responsible language for understanding utterances in conversations, since Korean speakers uttered more semantic formulas than Japanese speakers. And to the second research question, Korean speakers uttered the semantic formulas REASON, ADDRESS TERM, ADVERB, INTERJECTION, and COMPENSATION in apologies significantly more than Japanese speakers. Finally, to the third research question, it was found that daily use of American English influenced the use of Japanese and Korean by their respective native speakers especially in the case of Japanese.

Request-type discourse by Japanese and Korean university students are discussed in the next chapter.

Chapter 5

Request Discourse by Japanese and Korean University Students

5.1 General Account

In the present chapter, the differences between Japanese and Korean with respect to the responsibility for understanding utterances are examined to demonstrate the hypothesis that Japanese is a listener-responsible language and Korean is a speaker-responsible language in requests as well as in apologies (Chapter 4). The DCT (Discourse Completion Test) was completed by Japanese and Korean university students who live in their own countries and who live in the United States of America. It was found that Korean speakers produce many more utterances (semantic formulas) and convey more information per utterance to the interlocutor than Japanese speakers. Particularly, Korean speakers uttered the semantic formulas REASON, ADVERB, ADDRESS TERM, and INTERJECTION more than Japanese in apologies or requests. Furthermore, it was found that Japanese university students who live in the U.S. uttered more semantic formulas than Japanese university students who live in Japan.

5.2 Introduction

In this chapter, the conversations by university students are examined in order to clarify that Japanese is a listener-responsible language and Korean is a speaker-responsible language in terms of making requests. Also, whether or not the responsibility for understanding utterances in requests is influenced by the daily use of English, which is classified as a speaker-responsible-language, is examined.

Three research questions are addressed:

> (1) Is the total number of semantic formulas different between Japanese and Korean in requests? Do Korean university students utter more semantic formulas than Japanese university students?
> (2) In utterances in a corresponding request situation, different semantic formulas are used in Japanese and Korean to help the listener understand the situation. What semantic formulas are preferred in Japanese and Korean, respectively?
> (3) Can the acquisition of English or daily use of English influence the ways Japanese and Korean speakers use their native language?

5.3   Data Analysis

The DCT, which is used in the present research and has been translated from Japanese and Korean into English, is shown below:

> You are visiting a professor to submit your term paper. However, the professor is saying that your term paper will not be accepted because the deadline has passed already.
>
> | |
> |---|
> | Professor: "The deadline was the day before yesterday."
You: (   )
Professor: "No, you don't have to apologize."
You: (   )
Professor: "If I accept your term paper, it would be unfair to the other students." |

Table 5-1 and table 5-2 shows the semantic formulas used with respect to the amount of information in utterances in the first turn and the second turn, respectively. Based on Blum-Kulka *et al.* (1989), these semantic formulas were made after considering the purpose of the present research. ADVERB and INTERJECTION occur before or after the APOLOGY expressions in the first turn. Since the semantic formula REQUEST was mainly uttered in the second turn by informants, ADVERB and INTERJECTION, which are used for semantic formula APOLOGY, were not counted.

Table 5-1. Semantic formulas and examples in the first turn

	Semantic formulas	Examples
1	APOLOGY	"I am sorry."
2	FACT	"I am late."
3	REASON	"I was sick."
4	ADVERB	"(I am) really (sorry)."
5	ADDRESS TERM	"Professor."
6	INTERJECTION	"Oh, (sorry)."
7	REQUEST	"Please accept my paper."
8	OTHERS	"I understand."

Table 5-2. Semantic formulas and examples in the second turn

	Semantic formulas	Examples
1	APOLOGY	"I am sorry."
2	FACT	"I am late."
3	REASON	"I was sick."
4	PROMISE	"I will not hand in papers late again."
5	ADDRESS TERM	"Professor."
6	SUGGESTION	"Why don't you deduct points from the grade?"
7	REQUEST	"Please accept my paper."

5.4 Results

All the results in the present chapter are expressed in percentages because the number of participants is different in each group. In addition to the statistical analyses, a two-way ANOVA was used to show whether or not there were significant differences in the total amount of information depending on the speaker's native language, gender or influence of English. Also, the MCT (Multiple Comparison Test) was used if there was a significant difference of interaction using Ryan's method. The statistical significance level is 5% in the present chapter.

5.4.1 The First Turn of Request-type Discourse
(1) Comparison between Japanese and Korean University Students

Table 5-3 indicates the total amount of information per semantic formula in the first turn for JU and KU. As shown in table 5-3, KU uttered more semantic formulas than JU in all categories except OTHERS in the first turn. The ANOVA revealed that the amount of Korean information was significantly higher than Japanese information with respect to the semantic formulas FACT, ADDRESS TERM, INTERJECTION and REQUEST.

As for the semantic formula APOLOGY, a significant difference was found between female students and male students. Female students uttered APOLOGY significantly more than male students.

(2) Influence of Daily Use of English

Table 5-4 shows the total amount of information per semantic formula in the first turn of JU, KU, JIU, and KIU.

Significant differences were found for the semantic formulas REASON, INTERJECTION, and REQUEST because of the main effect of using English in daily conversation (living in the U.S.). The results of the MCT revealed that JIU and KIU's total amount of information is significantly higher than JU and KU's with respect to REASON and REQUEST. In comparing the two Japanese groups, JIU's results are much higher than JU for all of the semantic formulas except ADVERB and ADDRESS TERM. The gaps between JU and JIU regarding semantic formulas ADVERB (4 points) and ADDRESS TERM (1 point) were not significant.

5.4.2 The Second Turn of Request-type Discourse
(1) Comparison between Japanese and Korean University Students

Table 5-5 shows the total amount of information of JU and KU. Regarding nationality, KU uttered REASON, PROMISE, and ADDRESS TERM significantly more than JU. JU's total amount of information is significantly higher than KU's for OTHERS. There is one significant difference between female students' and male students' results relating to REASON: KMU uttered REASON significantly more than KFU in the second turn.

Table 5-3. Total amount of information in the first turn of JU and KU

		Female	Male	χ^2 ANOVA (two way)	χ^2		by arcsin asin Post hoc analysis
1	JU	100.0	96.4	Nationality	0.00		
	KU	100.0	96.6	Gender	5.77	*	FU > MU
				Interaction	0.00		
2	JU	8.7	12.7	Nationality	4.44	*	JU > KU
	KU	21.4	24.1	Gender	0.38		
				Interaction	0.04		
3	JU	15.2	12.7	Nationality	1.21		
	KU	23.8	17.2	Gender	0.57		
				Interaction	0.09		
4	JU	10.9	7.2	Nationality	2.98		
	KU	19.0	17.2	Gender	0.32		
				Interaction	0.07		
5	JU	0.0	1.8	Nationality	17.26	*	KU > JU
	KU	9.5	20.7	Gender	3.51		
				Interaction	0.02		
6	JU	0.0	0.0	Nationality	61.68	*	KU > JU
	KU	35.7	31.0	Gender	0.10		
				Interaction	0.10		
7	JU	0.0	0.0	Nationality	39.26	*	KU > JU
	KU	23.8	20.7	Gender	0.06		
				Interaction	0.06		
8	JU	13.0	16.4	Nationality	0.11		
	KU	11.9	13.8	Gender	0.24		
				Interaction	0.02		

Note: *p<0.05, Unit: %, 1: Apology, 2: Fact, 3: Reason, 4: Adverb, 5: Address term, 6: Interjection, 7: Request, 8: Others, JU: Japanese university students, KU: Korean university students, FU: female university students, MU: male university students.

Table 5-4. Total amount of information in the first turn of JU, KU, JIU, and KIU

		JU	KU		χ^2 ANOVA (two way) by arcsin asin χ^2		Post hoc analysis
1	JU/KU	98.0	98.6	English	0.05		
	JIU/KIU	100.0	94.8	Nationality	2.42		
				Interaction	3.63		
2	JU/KU	10.9	22.5	English	1.46		
	JIU/KIU	35.3	12.1	Nationality	0.86		
				Interaction	10.89	*	JIU/KIU : JIU > KIU
3	JU/KU	13.9	21.1	English	7.64	*	JIU/KIU > JU/KU
	JIU/KIU	35.3	31.0	Nationality	0.14		
				Interaction	1.12		
4	JU/KU	8.9	17.2	English	0.01		
	JIU/KIU	5.9	20.7	Nationality	7.00	*	KU/KIU > JU/JIU
				Interaction	0.59		
5	JU/KU	1.0	14.1	English	2.72		
	JIU/KIU	0.0	6.9	Nationality	17.16	*	KU/KIU > JU/JIU
				Interaction	0.02		
6	JU/KU	0.0	33.8	English	5.90	*	
	JIU/KIU	0.0	8.6	Nationality	47.71	*	JIU/KIU : KIU > JIU
				Interaction	5.90	*	JU/KU : KU > JU
7	JU/KU	0.0	22.5	English	6.61	*	JIU/KIU > JU/KU
	JIU/KIU	5.9	31.0	Nationality	39.88	*	KU/KIU > JU/JIU
				Interaction	1.26		
8	JU/KU	14.9	12.7	English	1.48		
	JIU/KIU	20.6	19.0	Nationality	0.15		
				Interaction	0.01		

Note: *p<0.05, Unit: %, 1: Apology, 2: Fact, 3: Reason, 4: Adverb, 5: Address term, 6: Interjection, 7: Request, 8: Others, JU: Japanese university students, KU: Korean university students, JIU: Japanese international university students who live in the U.S., KIU: Korean international university students who live in the U.S.

Table 5-5. Total amount of information in the second turn of JU and KU

		Female	Male	χ^2 ANOVA (two way) by arcsin asin	χ^2		Post hoc analysis
1	JU	10.9	12.7	Nationality	0.62		
	KU	11.9	20.7	Gender	0.89		
				Interaction	0.35		
2	JU	13.0	5.5	Nationality	0.00		
	KU	4.8	13.8	Gender	0.03		
				Interaction	3.47		
3	JU	2.2	5.5	Nationality	34.47	*	KU > JU
	KU	26.2	48.3	Gender	4.14	*	KU: KMU > FMU
				Interaction	0.83		
4	JU	2.2	1.8	Nationality	5.43	*	KU > JU
	KU	4.8	17.2	Gender	1.51		
				Interaction	1.99		
5	JU	0.0	0.0	Nationality	27.81	*	KU >JU
	KU	9.5	24.1	Gender	1.63		
				Interaction	1.63		
6	JU	4.3	5.5	Nationality	0.66		
	KU	14.3	3.4	Gender	1.24		
				Interaction	2.16		
7	JU	82.6	85.5	Nationality	9.38	*	KU > JU
	KU	97.6	96.6	Gender	0.00		
				Interaction	0.20		
8	JU	19.6	16.4	Nationality	17.45	*	JU > KU
	KU	4.8	0.0	Gender	2.81		
				Interaction	1.31		

Note: *p<0.05, Unit: %, 1: Apology, 2: Fact, 3: Reason, 4: Promise, 5: Address term, 6: Suggestion, 7: Request, 8: Others, JU: Japanese university students, KU: Korean university students, KMU: Korean male university students, KFU: Korean female university students.

Table 5-6. Total amount of information in the second turn of JU, KU, JIU, and KIU

		J	K		χ^2 ANOVA (two way) by arcsin asin		Post hoc analysis
					χ^2		
1	JU/KU	11.9	14.1	English	76.22	*	J: JIU>JU
	JIU/KIU	23.5	10.3	Nationality	83.06	*	IU: JIU>KIU
				Interaction	92.28	*	
2	JU/KU	8.9	7.7	English	6.47	*	
	JIU/KIU	20.6	19.0	Nationality	0.10		
				Interaction	0.00		
3	JU/KU	4.0	32.1	English	0.22		J: JIU>JU
	JIU/KIU	14.7	20.7	Nationality	13.03	*	U: KU>JU
				Interaction	5.87	*	
4	JU/KU	2.0	9.0	English	1.82		
	JIU/KIU	5.9	13.8	Nationality	5.03	*	
				Interaction	0.04		
5	JU/KU	0.0	14.1	English	3.66		K: KU>KIU
	JIU/KIU	0.0	1.7	Nationality	15.05	*	U: KU>JU
				Interaction	3.66		
6	JU/KU	5.0	9.0	English	2.95		
	JIU/KIU	2.9	1.7	Nationality	0.09		
				Interaction	0.81		
7	JU/KU	84.2	88.5	English	2.33		J: JIU>JU
	JIU/KIU	97.1	86.2	Nationality	1.22		IU: JIU>KIU
				Interaction	4.20	*	
8	JU/KU	17.8	2.6	English	3.45		K: KIU>KU
	JIU/KIU	14.7	19.0	Nationality	2.64		U: JU>KU
				Interaction	6.21	*	

Note: *p<0.05, Unit: %, 1: Apology, 2: Fact, 3: Reason, 4: Promise, 5: Address Term, 6: Suggestion, 7: Request, 8: Others, U: university students, IU: International university students, JU: Japanese university students, KU: Korean university students, JIU: Japanese international university students who live in the U.S., KIU: Korean international university students who live in the U.S., K:Korean, J:Japanese,

(2) Influence of Daily Use of English

Table 5-6 below shows the results of ANOVA for the total amount of information in the second turn.

JU and JIU showed statistically significant differences in the semantic formulas APOLOGY, REASON, and REQUEST. In other words, JIU uttered APOLOGY, REASON, and REQUEST significantly more than JU. In regards to the results of KU and KIU, KU uttered ADDRESS TERM significantly more than KIU, however KIU uttered OTHERS significantly more than KU.

5.5 Discussion

The results show that Japanese and Korean have different features in their conversational structure associated with the responsibility for understanding utterances, though there are similarities in their writing styles. It suggests that a reader-responsible language does not have to be a listener-responsible language. Based on a comparison of both languages, Japanese is a listener-responsible language while Korean is a speaker-responsible language on the conversation level.

In terms of *delayed introduction of purpose*, Hinds (1990) and Takigawa (2006) pointed out that Japanese speakers and writers state their purpose at the end of essays and conversations. The results of the DCT taken by JU in the present chapter support their claim. No JU used the semantic formula REQUEST, which is their real purpose, in the first turn with the professor, instead they apologized. However, 22.5% of KU uttered the semantic formula REQUEST in the apology in the first turn. In addition, KU uttered the semantic formula REQUEST more than JU in the second turn. In others words, it could be said that Japanese is both a reader-responsible and a listener-responsible language, while Korean is a reader-responsible language and a speaker-responsible language.

As shown clearly in the results of the total amount of information above, KU tends to explain their situation positively, while JU leaves the understanding of the situation to the interlocutors. As for the semantic formula REASON, KU tried to explain their situation to the listener actively while JU did not.

Eom (2001) cited Brown & Levinson (1987) and pointed out that Japanese people tend to use *negative strategies* while Korean people tend to use *positive strategies* like American English native speakers in requests. Eom (2001) found that Japanese speakers use apology and Korean speakers use reason expressions as explanations (Eom used the Japanese term *iiwake* for apology, explanation, promise, reason etc. in her study, for example, though its original meaning is "excuse") in requests. The results of Eom (2001) in regards to the use of reason as a strategy in requests is the same as the present chapter: that Korean speakers uttered REASON more than Japanese speakers. Also, Eom (2001) pointed out that female speakers utter more explanations (*iiwake*) than male speakers both in Japanese and Korean. As described above, apology, explanation, promise, reason etc. included an explanation. In terms of apology, the results of Eom (2001) that female speakers utter more apologies than male speakers both in Japan and Korea also support the results of the first turn. However, male Japanese and Korean speakers uttered more apology expressions than female speakers even though there was no significant difference in the second turn. It suggests that semantic formulas should be compared on the discourse level, and not just on the sentence level between Japanese and Korean in requests. Wada *et al.* (2010) compared the differences in requests between Japanese native speakers and Korean Japanese learners, and pointed out that the amount of information given by Korean speakers which explains the speaker's situation is more than that given by Japanese speakers.

Kondo & Taniguchi (2007) compared the apology strategies between Japanese and American English speakers. According to them, if someone gave a reason for their apology, Japanese listeners take the reason as a "defense", while American speakers regard it as a "polite explanation" in apologies. The tendency of KU to give a reason for their apology in the results is similar to that of American speakers.

The finding that JIU and KIU uttered REQUEST, which is the purpose of the conversation, and REASON significantly more than JU and KU in the first turn is interesting. In the second turn, JIU uttered APOLOGY, REASON, and REQUEST significantly more than JU. It shows that the daily use of English may have influenced their way of speaking in Japanese and Korean.

It was found that KU often used ADDRESS TERM in the conversation, while no JU used ADDRESS TERM. Regarding the use of address terms in conversation, the results of this study confirm the claim of Yoon (2008) that Korean people use address terms as *contextualization cues* more frequently in conversations compared to Japanese people. In the present study, many KU uttered "Professor" to attract the listener's interest and make sure that the relationship between the speaker (student who is submitting a term paper and wants a degree) and the listener (who may accept the student's term paper even if it was late) is clear and established. There are several studies which reveal that Korean speakers use more address terms as a request strategy compared to Japanese speakers (Yoo, 2008; Wada *et al.*, 2010). According to Wada *et al.* (2010), Korean speakers use address terms to preface requests especially when the interlocutor is older than the speaker. Since the interlocutor is a professor who might be older than the speaker in the present chapter, it will be discussed whether the use of address terms as a strategy in requests is used in Korean or not in Chapter 7 of this book by analyzing office workers' conversations with their boss, colleague, and subordinate.

The percentage of KIU who used ADDRESS TERM is lower than KU. It is usual to call a professor just "professor" without his/her last or first name in Korea and Japan, however it may not be normal to use this address term in the U.S. This might be one of the reasons why KIU did not use as many address terms as KU. Also, the fact that the average ages of the groups were different could be a reason for this phenomenon.

The expression "~te-shimau" in Japanese conveys "by accident or not on purpose". Many Japanese informants used "Okurete shimau; I am late by accident" instead of explaining the reason in detail, because they expected the interlocutor to understand that the speaker was not late on purpose and there were reasons for the delay. A Korean expression "~hay-peylita" means "~te-shimau" in Japanese. Few Korean informants in the present study used the expression "~ hay-peylita" to show that they were late by accident, and as shown in the results they tried to explain the reasons.

5.6 Conclusions

The present research set out to investigate the differences between Japanese and Korean speakers' responsibility for the understanding of utterances in a conversation. The experiment was carried out to compare the amount of information uttered, which is helpful for listeners in corresponding situations in both Japanese and Korean. To the first research question, the results of this chapter suggest that Korean should be classified as a speaker-responsible language for understanding in conversations, since Korean speakers produce many more utterances and convey more information per utterance to the interlocutor than Japanese speakers. To the second research question, Korean speakers uttered the semantic formulas REASON, ADVERB, ADDRESS TERM, and INTERJECTION more than Japanese in apologies or requests. Finally, to the third research question, speaker-responsibility and listener-responsibility correlate with daily use of American English, especially in the case of Japanese university students.

The current research will help clarify the possible misunderstandings between Japanese and Korean speakers, owing to the different responsibility for understanding in a conversation, and could promote more efficient foreign language teaching. Korean learners of the Japanese language and Japanese learners of the Korean language not only feel that it is easier to learn Japanese and Korean, respectively, but also acquire each language faster than learners from other countries because of the cultural and linguistic similarities. However, the similarities in grammatical structures, writing patterns and cultures do not assure similarities in discourse style.

Therefore, teaching Japanese (to Korean learners) and Korean (to Japanese learners) as foreign languages should be carried out while recognizing that the differences in the responsibility for understanding utterances between Japanese and Korean could hinder communication, especially for advanced learners. In addition, the results of the Japanese international students who live in the United States of America showed that they tend to take more responsibility for the understanding of utterances while speaking even when they speak in their native language. It will also be helpful to use this information in English class with Japanese or Korean students, or native English speakers studying Japanese or Korean.

In the next chapter, I will discuss the differences in the responsibility for understanding utterances between Japanese and Korean by analyzing the conversations of office workers.

Chapter 6

Apology Discourse by Japanese and Korean Office Workers

6.1 General Account

The present chapter aims to demonstrate that Korean can be seen as a speaker-responsible language on the level of conversation, though it is usually categorized as a listener-responsible language similar to Japanese. A descriptive questionnaire was conducted to find out how Korean speakers try to help their listeners' understand their utterances. The results illustrate that Korean is a speaker-responsible language, Japanese is a listener-responsible language, and both Japanese and Korean speakers tend to take responsibility for the understanding of utterances toward a listener of higher social status, compared to a listener of lower social status. Moreover, Japanese female and Korean male office workers utter more semantic formulas to facilitate their interlocutor's understanding than Japanese male and Korean female speakers, respectively.

6.2 Introduction

In this chapter, Japanese and Korean office workers' apology discourses were compared in order to demonstrate that Japanese is a listener-responsible language and Korean is a speaker-responsible language. In Chapter 4 of this book, the conversations by university students were compared and it was found that Korean university students' total amount of information is higher than that of Japanese university students' in apologies. Korean speakers tend to give the interlocutor information to convey their intention clearly, while Japanese speakers tend to leave the understanding of utterances to the interlocutor. The hypothesis is examined through different social groups in Japan and Korea in order to confirm the results of Chapter 4 and also to confirm the correlation between responsibility for the understanding of utterances and the status of the interlocutor.

The hypothesis posited is that Japanese is a listener-responsible language and Korean is a speaker-responsible language on the level of conversation. It is important to keep in mind that Japanese and Korean cultures value age and status greatly. Thus, the way Japanese or Korean people talk to a person depends on the relationship between the speaker and the listener. Three research questions arise:

> (1) Are the number of semantic formulas that Japanese and Korean people use different in apologies?
> (2) In utterances in a corresponding situation, different semantic formulas are used in Japanese and Korean to help the listener understand the situation. What semantic formulas are preferred in Japanese and Korean, respectively?
> (3) How does the relationship between the speaker and the listener influence the amount of semantic formulas uttered in the same situation in Japanese and Korean?
> (4) Are there any gender differences between Japanese and Korean speakers in the above research questions?

6.3 Data Analysis

A descriptive questionnaire was conducted to compare quantity and sentence-types of utterances and how their differences can be relevant in terms of contribution to the conversation and to the interpretation of the speaker's intention in Japanese and Korean conversations. The questionnaire, which has been translated from Japanese and Korean into English, is shown below:

> You are about 10 minutes late for a business meeting. What do you say to the following people?

```
Boss: (                                                      )
Colleague: (                                                 )
Subordinate: (                                               )
```

Table 6-1 shows the semantic formulas used with respect to the amount of information in utterances.

Table 6-1. Semantic formulas and examples

	Semantic formulas	Examples
1	APOLOGY	"I am sorry."
2	FACT	"I am late."
3	REASON	"I had to do something important."
4	ADVERB	"(I am) really (sorry)."
5	INTERJECTION	"Oh, (I am sorry)."
6	PROMISE	"I will not be late again."
7	COMPENSATION	"I will buy you a cup of coffee later."
8	SUGGESTION	"Let's start the meeting."
9	OTHERS	"Everyone makes mistake."

Based on Blum-Kulka *et al.* (1989), these semantic formulas were made after considering the purpose of the present study. ADVERB and INTERJECTION stand for what is used right in front or right after APOLOGY expressions.

6.4 Results

6.4.1 Comparison between Japanese and Korean Office Workers

All the results are expressed in percentages because the number of participants is different in each group. In addition to the statistical analyses, ANOVA was used to show whether or not there are significant differences in the total amount of information depending on the speaker's native language, gender, and the social relationship between the speaker and the listener.

Table 6-2 represents the total amount of information per semantic formula in apologies to a boss, colleague or subordinate by Japanese and Korean office workers. An ANOVA was conducted in order to determine if Japanese and Korean speakers' amount of semantic formulas varied depending on the relationship with their conversational partners.

There were four significant differences between Japanese and Korean office workers' results relating to the semantic formulas APOLOGY, REASON, ADVERB, INTERJECTION, PROMISE, COMPENSATION, and SUGGESTION: Korean speakers uttered the semantic formulas more than Japanese speakers except for APOLOGY and ADVERB. First, Korean speakers uttered the semantic formula REASON more than Japanese speakers to a boss or colleague. Second, the total amount of Korean speakers' information given in INTERJECTION was significantly higher than Japanese speakers in the cases where they were speaking to a colleague or subordinate. Third, Korean speakers uttered the semantic formula COMPENSATION significantly more than Japanese speakers to a subordinate. Finally, Korean speakers uttered the semantic formula SUGGESTION to a colleague and subordinate more than Japanese speakers.

On the other hand, Japanese office workers uttered the semantic formulas APOLOGY and ADVERB significantly more to a subordinate or boss than Korean office workers did.

Regarding the relationships between speakers and listeners, there were three significant differences (APOLOGY, INTERJECTION, SUGGESTION) in Korean and two significant differences (ADVERB, INTERJECTION) in Japanese. The amount of information of the semantic formula APOLOGY had an inverse relationship to the semantic formula SUGGESTION: the use of the semantic formula APOLOGY increased significantly if the speaker was talking to a subordinate or boss compared to a colleague, while the use of SUGGESTION decreased significantly when comparing the same relationships. In terms of the semantic formula INTERJECTION, the amount used with a colleague or subordinate was significantly higher than that used with a boss in Korean, while INTERJECTION was used with a boss significantly more than was used with a colleague or subordinate in Japanese. Also, the amount of information given in ADVERB to a boss was significantly more than to a colleague or subordinate in Japan.

6.4.2   Comparison between Japanese Female and Male Office Workers

Table 6-3 shows the total amount of information uttered by male and female

Table 6-2. Total amount of information by Japanese and Korean offices workers in apologies

		Japanese	Korean		χ^2 ANOVA (two way) by arcsin asin		Post hoc analysis
					χ^2		
1	Boss	97.6	100.0	Relationship	9.07	*	K:B>C>S
	Colleague	97.6	97.5	Nationality	0.01		
	Subordinate	95.2	85.0	Interaction	4.53	*	S:J>K
2	Boss	78.6	75.0	Relationship	0.88		
	Colleague	73.8	77.5	Nationality	0.41		
	Subordinate	76.2	65.0	Interaction	1.14		
3	Boss	9.5	32.5	Relationship	1.79		
	Colleague	11.9	30.0	Nationality	11.15	*	B/C: K>J
	Subordinate	9.5	17.5	Interaction	1.28		
4	Boss	28.6	10.0	Relationship	13.95	*	J:B>C/S, K:B>S
	Colleague	4.8	7.5	Nationality	0.91		
	Subordinate	2.4	2.5	Interaction	4.17	*	B:J>K
5	Boss	2.4	0.0	Relationship	1.75		
	Colleague	0.0	12.5	Nationality	6.38	*	C/S:K>J
	Subordinate	0.0	7.5	Interaction	12.61	*	J:B>C/S, K:C/S>B
6	Boss	0.0	7.5	Relationship	4.20	*	K:B>C/S
	Colleague	0.0	0.0	Nationality	2.10		
	Subordinate	0.0	0.0	Interaction	4.20	*	B:K>J
7	Boss	0.0	0.0	Relationship	2.20		
	Colleague	0.0	2.5	Nationality	4.03		
	Subordinate	0.0	5.0	Interaction	2.20		
8	Boss	0.0	0.0	Relationship	11.30	*	K:S>B/C
	Colleague	0.0	5.0	Nationality	15.32	*	C/S:K>J
	Subordinate	0.0	25.0	Interaction	11.30	*	
9	Boss	2.4	0.0	Relationship	4.03	*	K:C/S>B
	Colleague	4.8	2.5	Nationality	1.11		
	Subordinate	4.8	5.5	Interaction	1.21		

Note: *p<0.05, Unit: %, 1: Apology, 2: Fact, 3: Reason, 4: Adverb, 5: Interjection, 6: Promise, 7: Compensation, 8: Suggestion, 9: Others, J: Japanese, K: Korean, B: Boss, C: Colleague, S: Subordinate speakers in Japanese.

Second, female office workers uttered the semantic formula FACT significantly more than male speakers. Third, female office workers uttered the semantic formula ADVERB significantly more to a boss than a colleague or subordinate and male office workers uttered the semantic formula ADVERB significantly more to a boss, colleague, or subordinate. Finally, male speakers uttered the semantic formula OTHERS significantly more than female speakers.

6.4.3 Comparison between Korean Female and Male Office Workers

Table 6-4 shows the amount of information per semantic formula by male and female Korean speakers. The ANOVA revealed significant differences regarding the relationships between the speaker and listener and gender of the speaker for the semantic formulas APOLOGY, INTERJECTION, PROMISE, COMPENSATION, and SUGGESTION in the responses by Korean office workers in apologies.

First, both Korean female and male office workers uttered the semantic formula APOLOGY significantly more to a boss or colleague than a subordinate. Second, Korean female office workers uttered the semantic formula INTERJECTION significantly more to a colleague than a boss, and Korean male office workers uttered the semantic formula INTERJECTION significantly more to a colleague or subordinate than a boss. Third, for the semantic formula PROMISE, both female and male office workers' total amount of information was significantly higher toward a boss than a colleague or subordinate. Fourth, Korea male office workers uttered the semantic formula COMPENSATON significantly more to a subordinate than a boss or colleague.

Also male speakers' total amount of information given in the semantic formula COMPENSATION was significantly higher than female speakers'. Finally, for the semantic formula SUGGESTION, female office workers uttered the semantic formula SUGGESTION significantly more to a subordinate than a boss or colleague, and male office workers uttered the semantic formula SUGGESTION significantly more to a colleague or subordinate than boss.

Table 6-3. Total amount of information by Japanese office workers in apologies

		Female	Male		χ^2 ANOVA (two way) by arcsin asin χ^2		Post hoc analysis
1	Boss	100.0	95.0	Relationship	0.26		
	Colleague	100.0	95.0	Gender	8.34	*	S:F>M
	Subordinate	100.0	90.0	Interaction	0.26		
2	Boss	100.0	55.0	Relationship	2.21		
	Colleague	90.9	55.5	Gender	33.01	*	B/C/S:F>M
	Subordinate	90.9	60.0	Interaction	3.16		
3	Boss	13.6	5.0	Relationship	0.26		
	Colleague	13.6	10.0	Gender	1.83		
	Subordinate	13.6	5.0	Interaction	0.26		
4	Boss	27.3	30.0	Relationship	19.07	*	F:B>C/S,M:B>C>S
	Colleague	4.5	5.0	Gender	0.41		
	Subordinate	4.5	0.0	Interaction	1.54		
5	Boss	0.0	5.0	Relationship	1.42		
	Colleague	0.0	0.0	Gender	0.71		
	Subordinate	0.0	0.0	Interaction	1.42		
6	Boss	0.0	7.5	Relationship	2.15		
	Colleague	0.0	0.0	Gender	1.07		
	Subordinate	0.0	0.0	Interaction	2.15		
7	Boss	0.0	0.0	Relationship	0.00		
	Colleague	0.0	0.0	Gender	0.00		
	Subordinate	0.0	0.0	Interaction	0.00		
8	Boss	0.0	0.0	Relationship	0.00		
	Colleague	0.0	0.0	Gender	0.00		
	Subordinate	0.0	0.0	Interaction	0.00		
9	Boss	0.0	5.0	Relationship	0.26		
	Colleague	0.0	10.0	Gender	10.54	*	C/S:M>F
	Subordinate	0.0	10.0	Interaction	0.26		

Note: *$p<0.05$, Unit: %, 1: Apology, 2: Fact, 3: Reason, 4: Adverb, 5: Interjection, 6: Promise, 7: Compensation, 8: Suggestion, 9: Others, F: Female, M: Male, B: Boss, C: Colleague, S: Subordinate

Table 6-4 Total amount of information by Korean office workers in apologies

		Female	Male		χ^2 ANOVA (two way) by arcsin asin χ^2		Post hoc analysis
1	Boss	100.0	100.0	Relationship	10.52	*	F/M:B/C>S
	Colleague	96.0	100.0	Gender	2.03		
	Subordinate	80.0	93.3	Interaction	1.02		
2	Boss	76.0	73.3	Relationship	2.49		
	Colleague	68.0	93.3	Gender	2.53		
	Subordinate	60.0	73.3	Interaction	2.58		
3	Boss	24.0	46.7	Relationship	2.66		
	Colleague	28.0	33.3	Gender	4.90		
	Subordinate	8.0	33.3	Interaction	1.43		
4	Boss	12.0	6.7	Relationship	2.65		
	Colleague	8.0	6.7	Gender	0.26		
	Subordinate	0.0	6.7	Interaction	2.65		
5	Boss	0.0	0.0	Relationship	11.50	*	F:C>B,M:C/S>B
	Colleague	8.0	20.0	Gender	1.48		
	Subordinate	4.0	13.0	Interaction	0.74		
6	Boss	8.0	6.7	Relationship	7.52	*	F/M:B>C/S
	Colleague	0.0	0.0	Gender	0.01		
	Subordinate	0.0	0.0	Interaction	0.02		
7	Boss	0.0	0.0	Relationship	2.56		
	Colleague	4.0	0.0	Gender	0.35		
	Subordinate	0.0	13.0	Interaction	6.27	*	M:S>B/C, S:M>F
8	Boss	0.0	0.0	Relationship	16.24	*	F:S>B/C,M:C/S>B
	Colleague	4.0	6.7	Gender	0.19		
	Subordinate	28.0	13.3	Interaction	1.22		
9	Boss	0.0	0.0	Relationship	1.89		
	Colleague	0.0	6.7	Gender	0.01		
	Subordinate	8.0	0.0	Interaction	5.64		

Note: *p<0.05, Unit: %, 1: Apology, 2: Fact, 3: Reason, 4: Adverb, 5: Interjection, 6: Promise, 7: Compensation, 8: Suggestion, 9: Others, F: Female, M: Male, B: Boss, C: Colleague, S: Subordinate

6.5 Discussion

6.5.1 Difference of Total Amount of Information by Japanese and Korean Office Workers

The results of the research on office workers above confirm the claim that Japanese is a listener-responsible language, while Korean is a speaker-responsible language in apologies from Chapter 4, which was examined by comparing Japanese and Korean university students' conversations. As shown in the results, Korean speakers tried to explain their situation to the listener actively. The results regarding the semantic formula REASON are the same. The ANOVA revealed that Korean speakers utter the semantic formula REASON more than Japanese speakers in both the cases of university students and office workers. It is interesting to note that the ANOVA revealed that Korean speakers utter the semantic formula REASON significantly more than Japanese speakers, even though the research methods used on university students and office workers were different. For university students, the reason why the participant was late for the appointment was given by explanation of the situation that the lecture finished late while, for office workers, the reason was not given.

It is interesting that many Japanese participants used "Okurete shimau" (I am late by accident) ("~te-shimau" in Japanese conveys "by accident" or "not on purpose") instead of explaining the reason in detail. By using this expression, Japanese listeners are expected to understand that the speakers were not late on purpose and there were specific reasons. There is the same expression "~te-shimau" in Korean "~e-belyessta". Korean speakers used the conclusive expression "~ta" instead of "~e-belyessta" in the corresponding situation as shown in the following example (emphasized by the author):

> J: "Okurete*shimatte* moshiwake gozaimasen."
> (I am sorry I am late (by accident).)
> K: Nucese coysonhapnita.
> (I am sorry I am late.)

In addition to the reason, Korean speakers uttered more semantic formulas, especially INTERJECTION, COMPENSATION and SUGGESTION than Japanese speakers to convey their intention to the interlocutors. For the semantic formulas INTERJECTION and COMPENSATION, the results of office workers were the same at the results of university students (Chapter 4) in apologies. The results here also support the results of research done on university students' use of apologies (in Chapter 4) in regards to semantic formulas INTERJECTION and COMPENSATION.

Regarding the function of interjections in conversation, Sadanobu (2005) pointed out that interjections are not only used to hold a turn in a conversation in Japanese, but also to express the emotions of the speaker. Yamane (2002) also analyzed the functions of interjections used in various discourses in Japanese and classified them into five groups. One of the functions is related to the suggestion of the emotional state of the speaker. Yoon (2009) compared the use of interjections and address terms between Japanese and Korean, and claimed that some of interjections and address terms are used as *contextualization cues* (Gumperz, 1982) in Japanese and Korean discourse. The results of the DCT and the descriptive questionnaire clearly show that interjections are used intentionally in a Korean conversation, rather than always spoken unconsciously as hesitation in a natural verbal conversation since Korean speakers wrote down the semantic formula INTERJECTION intentionally.

Blum-Kulka *et al.* (1989) introduced five potential strategies used for the apology speech act which includes the semantic formula COMPENSATION. Blum-Kulka *et al.* (1989) used the term "repair" instead of the term "compensation":

1. an IFID[1] (be sorry; apologize; regret; excuse etc);
2. an explanation or account of the cause which brought about the violation;
3. an expression of the speaker's responsibility for the offence;
4. an offer of repair and
5. a promise of forbearance   (Blum-Kulka *et al.*, 1989; 20)

The situation for the university students is that the speaker was late to meet a friend to see a movie, thus many Korean speakers offered the interlocutor a movie ticket or a box of popcorn which they could enjoy together. Similarly, Korean office workers offered a cup of coffee after the meeting to a coworker. In other words, whether or not the interlocutor needs it now, Korean speakers tend to offer compensation as part of the apology and convey their apologetic emotion. On the other hand, none of the Japanese university students responded using the semantic formula COMPENSATION.

Blum-Kulka *et al*. (1989) defined the *offer of repair* (compensation in the present study) as follows:

> *Offer of repair*. In situations where the damage or inconvenience which affected the hearer can be compensated for, the speaker can choose to offer repair in a specified or general manner, intending this as an apology; for example, 'I'll pay for the damage' in the case of an accident caused by the speaker is specific enough to count as an apology.
>
> (Blum-Kulka *et al*., 1989: 21)

None of the Japanese office workers responded using the semantic formula SUGGESTION which suggests starting the business meeting to the interlocutor. However, Korean office workers suggested starting the meeting by using the expression of "Let's~" to the interlocutor in order to show their apologetic feeling that the meeting was delayed because of themselves.

6.5.2 Correlation between the Total Amount of Information and the Relationship between the Speaker and Listener

In this section, the correlation between responsibility for understanding utterances and the relationship of the speaker and listener is examined. Japanese and Korean discourse is influenced by the relationship between the speaker and listener as reflected in corresponding honorific systems.

Uttering the semantic formula APOLOGY is the most important in apologies, and out of all the semantic formulas analyzed APOLOGY was uttered the most in both Japanese and Korean. However, the results show a difference in the total amount of APOLOGY used by Japanese and Korean, which depended on the relationship of the speaker and interlocutor. No matter who was the listener, Japanese speakers uttered APOLOGY to a boss, colleague, or subordinate equally. However, Korean office workers uttered APOLOGY to a boss significantly more than a colleague, and uttered APOLOGY to a colleague more than a subordinate. In terms of not saying "I am sorry." in Korean, Kim (1996) pointed out that Korean speakers utter just the fact that he or she is late instead of uttering the apologetic expression "I am sorry" to a very close friend. And according to Hong (2006), about 10% of Korean speakers said nothing to the person whose foot was stepped on by the speaker on the subway.

It could be suggested that Japanese speakers utter more apology expressions to people who are close friends or family members compared to Korean speakers from the results above. It is important to note that not only the distance between the speaker and listener, but also social status influences the apology speech act and the responsibility for understanding utterances in Korean.

Besides the semantic formula APOLOGY, the ANOVA revealed that Korean office workers uttered the semantic formula SUGGESTION the most to a subordinate, then colleague, finally boss. It is possible that the results are a reflection of Korean social convention in the workplace: for a lower status person to suggest starting an event such as a business meeting to a higher status or older person is avoided. If the person who was late for the business meeting is a boss, other office workers might be waiting for the boss instead of running the meeting. However, if the person who was late for the business meeting is a subordinate, the meeting might have already started.

Although there were no significant differences regarding semantic formulas FACT and REASON, Korean office workers uttered semantic formula FACT and REASON more to a boss or colleague than subordinate. As described above, uttering FACT and REASON are important devices in order to explain the reason for the speaker's apology and it helps the listener understand the utterances in apologies. In conclusion, taking responsibility for understanding utterances is closely connected with the relationship between the speaker and the listener in Korean.

One of the notable features in the results of Japanese speakers was that ADVERB was used significantly more to a boss than colleague or subordinate as the example below shows (emphasized by the author):

J: <u>Taihen</u> moshiwake gozaimasen. (to boss)
 (I am <u>really</u> sorry.)
J: Gomen. (to colleague)
 (I am sorry.)
J: Sumimasen. (to subordinate)
 (I am sorry.)

It could be assumed that Japanese speakers tend to take more responsibility for understanding utterances to a higher status listener than an equal or lower status listener in apologies than Korean speakers.

For the semantic formula INTERJECTION, the results are opposite in terms of the relationship between the speaker and listener in Japanese and Korean: Japanese uttered the semantic formula INTERJECTION only to a boss, while no Korean speakers uttered the semantic formula INTERJECTION to a boss. Korean speakers uttered the semantic formula INTERJECTION to only a colleague and subordinate.

6.5.3 Correlation between Total Amount of Information and Speaker's Gender

There is a negative correlation between Japanese and Korean office workers in terms of responsibility for understanding utterances by men and women in apologies. Japanese female speakers tend to take responsibility for the understanding of utterances by using the semantic formulas APOLOGY, FACT and REASON more than male speakers. On the other hand, Korean female speakers did not utter the semantic formulas above more frequently than male speakers. On the contrary, Korean male office workers uttered semantic formula REASON significantly more than Korean female office workers. The results of the present research were different to the results of the Japanese and Korean university students in chapter 4, which found that female speakers utter more than male speakers to convey their emotions actively, both in Japanese and Korean in apologies. It is possible that the positions of male and female office workers in the company and the conventions of companies are different in Japanese and Korean societies.

6.6 Conclusions

The present chapter set out to investigate the differences between Japanese and Korean speakers' responsibility for understanding utterances in apologies. The research was carried out to compare the number of utterances (helpful information for interlocutors), in corresponding situations in both Japanese and Korean. From what has been discussed above, the conclusion is as follows: Korean is a speaker-responsible language and Japanese is a listener-responsible language; both Japanese and Korean speakers tend to take responsibility for the understanding of utterances toward a higher social status listener compared to a lower social status listener; and Japanese female and Korean male office workers utter more semantic formulas to help their interlocutor's understanding than Japanese male and Korean female office workers in apologies, respectively.

I will discuss the request-type discourse by Japanese and Korean office workers in terms of responsibility for understanding utterances in the next chapter.

Endnotes

1. IFID (Illocutionary Force Indicating Device) is a category encompassing the explicit use of apology expressions that mean sorry, forgive me etc. (Blum-Kulka & Olshtain, 1984).

Chapter 7

Request Discourse by Japanese and Korean Office Workers

7.1 General Account

In this chapter, Japanese and Korean office workers' discourse was analyzed in order to compare the responsibility for understanding. The results illustrate that Korean is a speaker-responsible language and Japanese is a listener-responsible language. Not only did Korean office workers utter more semantic formulas than Japanese office workers but also used direct request expressions to convey their intentions clearly to the interlocutor. Both Japanese and Korean office workers uttered more semantic formulas APOLOGY and less direct request expressions to a boss than colleague or subordinate.

7.2 Introduction

In this chapter, the results with respect to office workers are examined in order to demonstrate that Japanese is a listener-responsible language and Korean is a speaker-responsible language in requests. In Chapter 4 of this book, the conversations of Japanese and Korean university students were compared and it was found that the total amount of information uttered by Korean university students is higher than Japanese university students' total amount of information in requests. Korean speakers tend to give the interlocutor much more information to convey their intention clearly, while Japanese tend to leave the understanding of utterances to the interlocutor. Furthermore, it was found that the results of Japanese speakers support the theory of *delayed introduction of purpose* (Hinds,

1990; Takigawa, 2006) but the results regarding Korean speakers do not support the explanation of Hinds (1990) outlined in Chapter 5.

The hypothesis is examined by looking at different social groups in Japan and Korea in order to confirm the results of Chapter 5, and also the correlation between responsibilities for the understanding of utterances and the status of the interlocutor are examined in the present chapter. The hypothesis is that Japanese is a listener-responsible language and Korean is a speaker-responsible language on the level of conversation. Furthermore, Japanese and Korean cultures greatly value age and status. Thus, the way Japanese or Korean people talk to a person depends on the relationship between the speaker and the listener. Four research questions arise:

> (1) Is the total number of semantic formulas used by Japanese speakers and Korean speakers in requests different? Do Korean office workers utter more semantic formulas than Japanese office workers in requests?
> (2) In utterances in a corresponding request situation, different semantic formulas can be used by Japanese and Korean office workers to help the listener understand the situation. What semantic formulas are preferred in Japanese and Korean, respectively?
> (3) How does the relationship between the speaker and the listener influence the amount of semantic formulas uttered in the same requests situation in Japanese and Korean?
> (4) Are there any gender differences between Japanese and Korean speakers in the above research questions?

7.3   Data Analysis

A descriptive questionnaire was conducted to compare the quantity of information and sentence-types of utterances in Japanese and Korean conversations, and how their differences can be relevant in terms of contribution to the conversation and to the interpretation of the speaker's intention. The questionnaire, which is used in the present study and has been translated from Japanese and Korean into English, is shown below:

> You want to ask your colleague, who is going to a convenience store, to buy a sandwich for you. What do you say to the following people?

Boss: (	)
Colleague: (	)
Subordinate: (	)

As described in Chapter 3 (Methodology), the participants of this chapter are 42 (20 males Mean age = 27.9 years, 22 females Mean age = 27.8 years) Japanese and 40 (15 males Mean age = 31.1 years, 25 females Mean age = 28.9 years) Korean office workers. However, some participants refused to complete the descriptive questionnaire since they thought that they would never ask a coworker to buy them a sandwich even if they were very hungry. Thus, the participants who answered that they would say nothing to the interlocutors were excluded from the analysis. Table 7-1 shows the proportions of participants who refused to complete the descriptive questionnaire.

Table 7-1. The proportions of Japanese and Korean workers who refused to complete the questionnaire

Request to	Japanese	Korean
Boss	31.0%(13)	21.4%(9)
Colleague	2.4%(1)	2.5%(1)
Subordinate	2.4%(1)	5.0%(2)

There are no large differences between Japanese and Korean office workers refusing to answer the questionnaire. However, the proportion of Japanese office workers who did not ask their boss to buy them a sandwich is higher than the proportion of Korean office workers.

Table 7–2 shows the semantic formulas used with respect to the amount of utterances in requests. Based on Blum-Kulka *et al.* (1989), these semantic formulas were made under consideration of the purpose of the present research. The semantic formula ADVERB stands for what is used right in front or right after the APOLOGY expressions.

Table 7-2. Semantic formulas and examples

	Semantic formulas	Examples
1	APOLOGY	"I am sorry."
2	REASON	"I have not eaten lunch yet."
3	REQUEST	"Can you buy a sandwich for me?"
4	SUBJUNCTIVE	"If you go to convenience store..."
5	PRECOMMITMENT	"Will you do me a favor?"
6	ADDRESS TERM	"Boss!"
7	ADVERB	"(I am) Really (sorry but will you buy me...?)"
8	OTHERS	"Where are you going?"

7.4 Results

7.4.1 Total Amount of Information by Japanese and Korean in Requests

7.4.1.1 Comparison between Japanese and Korean Office Workers

All the results are expressed in percentages because the number of Japanese and Korean participants was different. In addition to the statistical analyses, ANOVAs were used to show whether or not there are significant differences in the total amount of information depending on the speaker's native language, gender, or the social relationship between the speaker and the listener in requests.

Table 7-3 below represents the total amount of information per semantic formula in requests to a boss, colleague or subordinate between Japanese and Korean office workers.

Table 7-3. Total amount of information by Japanese and Korean office workers in requests

		Japanese	Korean	χ^2 ANOVA (two way) by arcsin asin	χ^2		Post hoc analysis
1	Boss	72.4	41.9	Relationship	17.6	*	J/K: B>C/S
	Colleague	48.8	10.3	Nationality	27.7	*	J>K
	Subordinate	43.9	15.8	Interaction	0.8		
2	Boss	31.0	32.3	Relationship	3.0		
	Colleague	17.1	25.6	Nationality	1.0		
	Subordinate	17.1	23.7	Interaction	0.3		
3	Boss	100.0	100.0	Relationship	1.2		
	Colleague	97.6	100.0	Nationality	0.6		
	Subordinate	100.0	100.0	Interaction	1.2		
4	Boss	31.0	45.2	Relationship	0.3		
	Colleague	34.1	38.5	Nationality	2.5		
	Subordinate	34.1	47.4	Interaction	0.4		
5	Boss	6.9	6.5	Relationship	4.8	*	K:B>C
	Colleague	2.4	0.0	Nationality	0.6		
	Subordinate	2.4	2.6	Interaction	1.2		
6	Boss	0.0	38.7	Relationship	3.2		
	Colleague	0.0	23.1	Nationality	56.9	*	K>J
	Subordinate	0.0	13.2	Interaction	3.2		
7	Boss	27.6	0.0	Relationship	6.5	*	J:B>C/S
	Colleague	4.9	0.0	Nationality	20.8	*	B/S:J>K
	Subordinate	2.4	0.0	Interaction	6.5	*	
8	Boss	6.9	0.0	Relationship	5.3	*	K:C/S>B
	Colleague	7.3	12.8	Nationality	0.0		
	Subordinate	2.4	13.2	Interaction	8.9	*	B:J>K, S:K>J

Note: *p<0.05, Unit: %, 1: Apology, 2: Reason, 3: Request, 4: Subjunctive, 5: Precommitment, 6: Address Term, 7: Adverb, 8: Others, J: Japanese, K: Korean, B: Boss, C: Colleague, S: Subordinate

An ANOVA was conducted in order to determine if Japanese and Korean speakers' amount of semantic formulas varied depending on the relationship with their conversational partners.

As Table 7-3 shows, for the semantic formulas APOLOGY, ADDRESS TERM, ADVERB, and OTHERS, the ANOVA revealed significant differences between Japanese and Korean speakers. Japanese office workers uttered APOLOGY and ADVERB significantly more than Korean office workers. Korean office workers uttered the semantic formula ADDRESS TERM significantly more than Japanese office workers. Japanese office workers uttered OTHERS significantly more than Korean office workers to a boss, while Korean office workers uttered OTHERS significantly more than Japanese when the interlocutor was a subordinate.

Regarding the relationship between the speaker and the listener, both Japanese and Korean office workers uttered the semantic formula APOLOGY significantly more to a boss than a colleague or subordinate. Japanese office workers uttered the semantic formula ADVERB significantly more to a boss than a colleague or subordinate, while no Korean office workers uttered ADVERB. Korean office workers uttered the semantic formula PRECOMMITMENT significantly more to a boss than a colleague. Korean office workers uttered OTHERS significantly more to a colleague or subordinate than a boss.

7.4.1.2　Comparison between Japanese Female and Male Office Workers

Table 7-4 represents the total amount of information per semantic formula by Japanese office workers in requests.

Table 7-4. Total amount of information by Japanese office workers in requests

		Female	Male		χ^2 ANOVA (two way) by arcsin asin		Post hoc analysis
					χ^2		
1	Boss	78.6	66.7	Relationship	7.78	*	F/M:B>C/S
	Colleague	54.5	42.1	Gender	2.91		
	Subordinate	54.5	31.6	Interaction	0.26		
2	Boss	42.9	20.0	Relationship	2.58		
	Colleague	18.2	15.8	Gender	1.18		
	Subordinate	18.2	15.8	Interaction	1.14		
3	Boss	100.0	100.0	Relationship	1.28		
	Colleague	100.0	94.7	Gender	0.64		
	Subordinate	100.0	100.0	Interaction	1.28		
4	Boss	35.7	26.7	Relationship	0.06		
	Colleague	40.9	26.3	Gender	2.00		
	Subordinate	40.9	26.3	Interaction	0.08		
5	Boss	0.0	13.3	Relationship	0.60		
	Colleague	4.5	0.0	Gender	0.04		
	Subordinate	4.5	0.0	Interaction	8.29	*	M:B>C/S,B: M>F
6	Boss	0.0	0.0	Relationship	0.00		
	Colleague	0.0	0.0	Gender	0.00		
	Subordinate	0.0	0.0	Interaction	0.00		
7	Boss	28.6	26.7	Relationship	17.27	*	F/M:B>C/S
	Colleague	9.1	0.0	Gender	3.52		
	Subordinate	4.5	0.0	Interaction	1.52		
8	Boss	0.0	13.3	Relationship	1.77		
	Colleague	4.5	10.5	Gender	6.22	*	B:M>F
	Subordinate	0.0	5.3	Interaction	1.20		

Note: *$p<0.05$, Unit: %, 1: Apology, 2: Reason, 3: Request, 4: Subjunctive, 5: Precommitment, 6: Address Term, 7: Adverb, 8: Others, F: Female, M: Male, B: Boss, C: Colleague, S: Subordinate

The ANOVA revealed that there were significant differences for the semantic formulas APOLOGY, PRECOMMITMENT, and ADVERB regarding the relationship between the speaker and the listener, and gender of the Japanese speaker. Both Japanese female and male office workers uttered APOLOGY and ADVERB significantly more to a boss than a colleague or subordinate. For the semantic formula PRECOMMITMENT, the total amount uttered by male office workers was higher than female office workers' when the listener was a boss. Also, male office workers uttered PRECOMMITMENT significantly more to a boss than a colleague or subordinate, while there was no significant difference depending on the relationship in the results of female office workers.

7.4.1.3 Comparison between Korean Female and Male Office Workers
Table 7-5 shows the total amount of information by Korean female and male office workers in requests. The ANOVA revealed that there were four semantic formulas (APOLOGY, PRECOMMITMENT, ADDRESS TERM, and OTHERS) which included significant differences depending on the relationship between the speaker and the listener or gender of the speakers.

First, Korean female office workers uttered the semantic formula APOLOGY significantly more to a boss than a colleague or subordinate. Male office workers uttered APOLOGY significantly more to a boss than a colleague, but there was no significant difference for female respondents between a boss and subordinate.

Table 7-5. Total amount of information by Korean office workers in requests

		Female	Male	χ^2 ANOVA (two way) by arcsin asin	χ^2		Post hoc analysis
1	Boss	40.0	45.5	Relationship	9.80	*	F:B>C/S,M:BC
	Colleague	4.0	21.4	Gender	2.52		
	Subordinate	12.0	23.1	Interaction	0.83		
2	Boss	25.0	45.5	Relationship	1.23		
	Colleague	28.0	21.4	Gender	0.18		
	Subordinate	24.0	23.1	Interaction	1.53		
3	Boss	100.0	100.0	Relationship	0.00		
	Colleague	100.0	100.0	Gender	0.00		
	Subordinate	100.0	100.0	Interaction	0.00		
4	Boss	50.0	36.4	Relationship	0.46		
	Colleague	32.0	50.0	Gender	0.23		
	Subordinate	44.0	53.8	Interaction	1.81		
5	Boss	5.0	9.1	Relationship	4.68	*	M:B>C/S
	Colleague	0.0	0.0	Gender	0.16		
	Subordinate	4.0	0.0	Interaction	1.37		
6	Boss	40.0	36.4	Relationship	5.38	*	F:B>C/S,M:B>S
	Colleague	16.0	35.7	Gender	0.63		
	Subordinate	12.0	15.4	Interaction	1.20		
7	Boss	0.0	0.0	Relationship	0.00		
	Colleague	0.0	0.0	Gender	0.00		
	Subordinate	0.0	0.0	Interaction	0.00		
8	Boss	0.0	0.0	Relationship	12.16	*	F/M:C/S>B
	Colleague	12.0	14.3	Gender	0.07		
	Subordinate	12.0	15.4	Interaction	0.04		

Note: *$p<0.05$, Unit: %, 1: Apology, 2: Reason, 3: Request, 4: Subjunctive, 5: Precommitment, 6: Address Term, 7: Adverb, 8: Others, F: Female, M: Male, B: Boss, C: Colleague, S: Subordinate

Second, male office workers uttered the semantic formula PRECOMMITMENT significantly more to a boss than a colleague or subordinate, while there was no significant difference between boss, colleague, and subordinate in the results of female office workers. Third, female office workers' total amount of the semantic formula ADDRESS TERM used with a boss was significantly higher than used with a colleague or subordinate. Male office workers' total amount of information given was significantly higher to a boss than to a subordinate for semantic formula ADDRESS TERM. Finally, both female and male office workers uttered OTHERS significantly more to a boss than a colleague or subordinate.

7.4.2 Sentence Types of Utterances in Requests between Japanese and Korean

The semantic formula REQUEST uttered by Japanese and Korean office workers was analyzed and classified into two types of expressions, direct and indirect. The direct expressions include a sentence that matches the speech act request directly, for example, "Kattekite kudasai" (Please buy it for me) in Japanese. The expression such as "Kattekite kuremasuka" (Can you buy it for me?) in Japanese was categorized as an indirect expression. A repeated measures ANOVA was conducted to investigate which types of utterances were used for the semantic formula REQUEST in Japanese and Korean, respectively.

Table 7-6 represents the types of sentences that are used for requests in Japanese and Korean.

There were significant differences with regard to the relationship (boss, colleague, and subordinate) and nationality (Japanese and Korean) in the types of the semantic formula REQUEST. Korean office workers used direct expressions

Table 7-6. Types of utterances of the semantic formula REQUEST by Japanese and Korean office workers in requests

		J	K	χ^2 ANOVA (two way) by arcsin asin		
					χ^2	Post hoc analysis
Direct	Boss	3.5	35.5	Relationship	24.1	* J/K: C/S>B
	Colleague	26.8	69.2	Nationality	36.6	* K>J
	Subordinate	31.7	65.8	Interaction	0.5	
Indirect	Boss	96.6	64.5	Relationship	24.1	* J/K: B>C/S
	Colleague	73.2	30.8	Nationality	36.6	* J>K
	Subordinate	68.3	34.2	Interaction	0.5	

Note: *p<0.05, Unit: %, J: Japanese, K: Korean, B: Boss, C: Colleague, S: Subordinate for a request significantly more than Japanese office workers no matter who was the interlocutor. And both Japanese and Korean speakers made indirect requests significantly more to a boss than a colleague or subordinate. There was no significant difference between the proportions of colleague and subordinate in both Japanese and Korean with reference to types of request expressions.

7.5 Discussion

The hypothesis is that Japanese is a listener-responsible language and Korean is a speaker-responsible language. Furthermore, the responsibility for understanding utterances correlates with the speaker's and listener's features such as social status and gender in requests was investigated. It was found that Korean office workers uttered more semantic formulas in order to convey their intentions clearly in requests, while Japanese office workers uttered fewer semantic formulas (except mentioning apologetic expressions) in requests. Also, it was found that Korean speakers used direct expressions for the semantic formula REQUEST significantly more than Japanese speakers.

In terms of the correlation between the responsibility for the understanding of utterances and the relationship with the interlocutors, both Japanese and Korean office workers tended to utter more semantic formulas to a person of higher position than to a person of lower or equal position. And both Japanese and Korean used an indirect expression for the semantic formula REQUEST significantly more to a boss than a colleague or subordinate. There was no significant difference between female and male office workers in the results.

The ANOVA revealed that Korean speakers' total amount of information was significantly higher than Japanese speakers' total amount of information for the semantic formula ADDRESS TERM. None of the Japanese respondents used address terms. It has been noted that Korean speakers use address terms as *contextualization cues* (Gumperz, 1982) in conversations (Yoon, 2008; 2009) and it has been found that Korean speakers use more address terms compared to Japanese speakers, especially in requests as shown in this book (Chapters 4 and 5). I pointed out that there are many variations of address terms within married couples and married couples tend to choose an address term depending on his or her emotion or the situation (Yoon, 2008). Inoue (2005) pointed out that address terms were used frequently after a conversation was started in English compared to Japanese, especially when the speaker wants to bring in intrusive subjects, change the framework of interpretation, or enhance the persuasive power of their utterances (Inoue, 2003; 2005). The results of the present study suggest that Korean and English tend to show similar features in terms of using address terms as *contextualization cues* in conversation. In addition, Blum-Kulka *et al.* (1989) pointed out that address terms are included in *alerters,* which are considered request sequences. She defined *alerters* as follows:

> ***Alerters.*** When preceding requests, alerters serve as attention-getters, and hence are equal in function to all verbal means used for this purpose. Coding of appellations (Title + surname/ Surname only, etc.) as well as semantic variations in items used ('daring, could you …' as opposed to 'you fool, why don't you …') Blum-Kulka *et al.* (1989: 17)

As shown in the example below, it is interesting that Korean office workers wrote down address terms expressly on the descriptive questionnaire such as "sangsa[1]-nim[2]" (boss), "kacang[3]-nim" (the head of a section), "senpay[4]-nim" (a senior), and "~~ -nim" (Mr. or Ms. ~~) to a boss, "chinku[5]" (friend), "ya[6]" (hey), "~~ -ya[7]" (hey, ~~) and "ei[8]" (hey) to a colleague, and "ya" (hey), "~~ -ya" (hey, ~~), and "~~ -ssi[9]" (Mr. or Ms. ~~) to a subordinate. It would be unnatural if a Korean worker called his or her boss using "sansan-nim" but the participants expressly made a temporary address term for the conversation without a real listener. For example, some participants used a special mark such as "~~".

Ka: "**~~ -nim**, coysonghantey sayntuwichi com puthaktulikeysssupnita."
(Mr. ~~, I am sorry but please grab a sandwich for me.   (To a boss)

Kb: "**Chinku**, papmekko olttay sayntuwichi com satacusam."
(Friend, grab me a sandwich on your way back to the office after lunch.)
(To a colleague)

Kc: "**~~-ya**, nayka ton culkey sayntuwichi com puthakhay."
(Hey ~~, I will give you some money, grab me a sandwich.)
(To a subordinate)

According to Wada *et al.* (2010), Korean speakers use address terms as a preface to a request especially when the interlocutor is older than the speaker.

In Chapter 5 of this book, it was pointed out that Korean university students addressed their interlocutor (professor), who might be older than the speaker, significantly more than Japanese university students did. Even though there was no significant difference, the proportion of the semantic formula ADDRESS TERM used by Korean office workers directly increased as the listener's status increased. Korean address terms used in companies have been studied before (Lim & Tamaoka, 2004; 2010). However, most of these studies have focused on how the address terms toward colleagues in Korean offices change depending on the listener's status or the situation: For example, if the use of address terms is formal or not, rather than considering the different speech acts or psychological facts of the speakers.

In Chapter 5, it was demonstrated that Korean university students uttered the semantic formulas REQUEST and REASON significantly more than Japanese university students in requests. Even though there was no significant difference, it was confirmed that Korean office workers uttered the semantic formula REASON more to colleagues and subordinates compared to Japanese office workers. It is remarkable that 100% of Korean office workers uttered the semantic formula REQUEST, which is the key semantic formula in the conversation, while some Japanese office workers did not use the semantic formula REQUEST for requests to a colleague.

Yoo (2008) claimed that both Japanese and Korean speakers explain reasons for requests. However, the results of this study show that there is no difference in the amount of information given in a reason for a request to a boss in Japanese and Korean, while Korean speakers give more reasons for requests to colleagues and subordinates.

Eom (2001) cited Brown & Levinson (1987) and pointed out that Japanese speakers tend to use *negative strategies* while Korean speakers tend to use *positive strategies* like American English native speakers in requests. Eom (2001) found that Japanese speakers use apologies and Korean speakers use reason expressions as explanations (Eom used the Japanese term *iiwake* for apology, explanation, promise, reason etc. in her study) in requests. The results of Eom (2001) in regards to the use of reasons as a strategy in requests are the same as the present chapter: that Korean speakers uttered reasons more than Japanese.

Also, Eom (2001) pointed out that female speakers utter more explanations (*iiwake*, i. e. "excuse") than male speakers both in Japanese and Korean. There was no significant difference between female and male speakers in either Japanese or

Korean associated with the uttering of the semantic formula REASON in the results. There is an inverse relationship between Japanese and Korean respondents in terms of gender: The proportion of REASON uttered by females is higher than males in Japanese, while the proportion of REASON uttered by males is higher than females in Korean. It is necessary to investigate the responsibility for understanding utterances by setting up new types of situations in requests in Japanese and Korean.

The ANOVA revealed that Japanese office workers uttered the semantic formulas APOLOGY and ADVERB, which is uttered right before and after the semantic formula APOLOGY, significantly more than Korean office workers. However, Korean university students uttered the semantic formula APOLOGY more than Japanese university students both in the first and second turns in requests (Chapter 5). One of the reasons for the noted differences between the university students' responses and the office workers' responses may be due to the fact that in the students' situation, they were the cause of the delay, while in the office workers' situation, the delay was caused by an outside source. The fact that Japanese office workers uttered the semantic formula APOLOGY more than Korean office workers may be caused by cultural differences between Japan and Korea, rather than responsibility for the understanding of utterances. The semantic formula APOLOGY is excluded from the request sequence of Blum-Kulka *et al.* (1989). Both Japanese and Korean office workers uttered the semantic formula APOLOGY significantly more to a boss than a colleague or subordinate.

In terms of apologetic expressions which are used in Japanese requests, it is assumed that the results were caused by the differences in discourse politeness between Japanese and Korean. Lai (2005) clarified that Japanese speakers tend to utter apologetic expressions no matter how the strength of burden of the request or the status of the listener is in comparison to Taiwanese Japanese learners.

Kumagai & Shinozaki (2006) also considered the apologetic expression in requests with reference to politeness in Japanese conversation and categorized the apologetic expression as an interpersonal consideration. Kumagai & Shinozaki (2006) found that older Japanese speakers tend to utter apologetic expressions more than younger Japanese speakers in requests.

This chapter also investigated the differences in sentence types for the semantic formula REQUEST in Japanese and Korean. The ANOVA revealed that Korean office workers used direct sentence types significantly more in conversations with all the interlocutors than Japanese office workers. Korean speakers tend to convey their intention by using a type of sentence which matches with the purpose of the utterances[10] (Yoon, 2009).

The ANOVA also demonstrated that both Japanese and Korean office workers used the direct semantic formula REQUEST with a colleague and subordinate significantly more than a boss. Taking responsibility for understanding utterances changes depending on the listener. For example, Korean speakers utter more semantic formulas to a person of higher status than a person of lower or equal status, however, they use indirect request expressions such as interrogative sentences. C. Kim (2006) pointed out that Japanese barely use direct sentence types of requests for example "~ te kudasai", while Korean frequently use direct sentence types of requests for example "~ e cuseyyo" toward older or higher status listeners in requests.

7.6 Conclusions

In conclusion, this research revealed that Korean and Japanese should be categorized differently (Japanese is a listener-responsible language and Korean is a speaker-responsible language) for the responsibility for understanding utterances even though both are currently categorized as listener-responsible languages (Hinds, 1987). It also found that both Korean and Japanese speakers manipulate the responsibility for the understanding of utterances, depending on the relationship between the speaker and the listener by giving more information or using different types of sentences. The correlation between responsibility for understanding utterances and politeness (*Pragmatic politeness*; Usami, 2002) should be addressed in future research in more diverse request situations using different participants.

Endnotes
1 boss, superior.
2 bound noun. (used after one's last name or first name) refers to him or her politely.
3 section chief (head).
4 a senior, a superior, an elder.
5 friend, buddy. usually refers to people who are the same age in Korea.
6 an address term used by a person who is older or the same age as a listener.
7 (used after the word, doesn't have final consonant) used when calling an animal or a person

who is younger or the same age.
8   a word used when calling a person who is a little far away. Used toward a person who is younger or the same age.
9   a word used when calling a person politely. Usually used toward a person who is younger or the same age.
10 In terms of sentence types of request expressions, the differences of linguistic explicity and language behavior between Japanese and Korean can also be considered. However, the present dissertation focuses on not only the sentence type, but also the amount of semantic formulas in order to compare responsibility for understanding utterances between Japanese and Korean.

Chapter 8

Conclusions

In this chapter, the results and findings are briefly summarized in relation to Hinds' theory which claims that both Japanese and Korean should be classified as reader/listener-responsible languages and contrastive discourse studies between Japanese and Korean in apologies and requests. Furthermore, the implications of this research for second or foreign language learning and intercultural communication are discussed.

This book set out to examine the hypothesis that Japanese is a listener-responsible language while Korean is a speaker-responsible language on the conversational level, even though Hinds (1987) claimed that both Japanese and Korean are listener-responsible languages. Experiments were carried out to compare the amount of information and the sentence types of utterances, in corresponding situations in both Japanese and Korean.

To the first research question (Are Japanese and Korean really both listener-responsible languages since it was found that they have similar rhetorical features, which are described as nonlinear or have indirect development of themes?), the results suggest that Korean should be classified as a speaker-responsible language for the understanding of utterances in conversations, since Korean speakers produce significantly more utterances and convey more information per utterance to the interlocutor than Japanese speakers. Furthermore, in terms of *delayed introduction of purpose* Hinds (1990) and Takigawa (2006) pointed out that Japanese speakers and writers state their purpose at the end of essays and conversations. As discussed in Chapter 5, it was found that Korean speakers tend to state their real purpose in earlier turns during discourse while Japanese speakers tend to avoid uttering their real purpose in earlier turns during discourse.

To the second research question (Is the amount of information different between Japanese and Korean in apologies and requests? Is the amount of semantic formulas influenced by different situations in Japanese and Korean, respectively? What semantic formulas are preferred in Japanese and Korean, respectively?), it was found that Korean speakers uttered the semantic formula REASON more than Japanese speakers in apologies and requests. In other words, Korean speakers give more information to help their listener understand utterances. The semantic formulas ADDRESS TERM and INTERJECTION were also uttered by Korean speakers more frequently than Japanese. Korean speakers give strong hints to convey their intention to the listener by using address terms or interjections, which work as *contextualization cues* (Gumperz, 1982) in conversations.

The sentence types of utterances were analyzed to investigate the third research question (Are the sentence types utterances that help convey the speakers' intention clearly different in Japanese and Korean? What sentences types are used frequently in similar situations in Japanese and Korean?). In apologies, it is hard to find any differences in sentence types whether they are direct or indirect. Instead of the differences of directness or indirectness, the results show that Korean university students added adverbs which emphasizes the speakers' feelings in apologetic expressions more than Japanese university students. The results of the research (chapter 6 and chapter 7) on office workers show that Korean office workers used adverbs for apologetic expressions to colleagues and subordinates. However, Japanese office workers used adverbs for apologetic expressions more than Korean office workers to a boss. In requests, as described in Chapters 5 and 7, it was found that Korean speakers use direct sentence type for request expressions more than Japanese speakers.

Finally, to the last research question (Is the responsibility for the understanding of utterances influenced by the speaker's features such as age, gender, occupation, residence, or the relationship between the speaker and listener?), there were several findings. The most interesting is that Japanese speakers' responsibility for the understanding of utterances is influenced by the daily use of, or acquisition of, English in the U.S. more than Korean speakers. In reference to politeness and the relationship between the speaker and the listener, the results of Japanese and Korean office workers show that the speaker who has higher status or is older will take less responsibility for the understanding of utterances compared to the speaker who has lower status or is younger. However, in spite of Korean speakers indicating a similar tendency as Japanese speakers, the results of Korean speakers suggest that different semantic formulas are used depending on the relationship between the speaker and listener to help the listener's understanding of utterances in Korean. This research, by closely examining the differences between female and male speakers in connection with the responsibility for the understanding of utterances, has revealed that female speakers generally tend to take more responsibility than male speakers for the understanding of utterances in both Japanese and Korean even though there are no significant differences. However, Korean female office workers tend to utter fewer semantic formulas than male speakers. It will be necessary to investigate the reasons for this in the future.

This research will help clarify the possible misunderstandings between Japanese and Korean speakers, owing to the difference in responsibility for understanding in a conversation, and promote more efficient second or foreign language teaching. Korean learners of the Japanese language and Japanese learners of the Korean language not only feel that it is easier to learn Japanese and Korean, respectively, but also acquire each language faster than learners from other countries because of the cultural and linguistic similarities between Japanese and Korean. However, the similarities in grammatical structures, writing patterns and cultures do not assure similarities in discourse style.

Therefore, teaching Japanese (to Korean learners) and Korean (to Japanese learners) as a foreign languages should be carried out while recognizing that the differences in the responsibility for understanding utterances between Japanese and Korean could hinder communication, especially for advanced learners. In addition, the results of the Japanese and Korean university students who live in the United States of America will also be helpful to teachers of English as a second or foreign language with Japanese or Korean students, or native English speakers studying Japanese or Korean as a second or foreign language.

References

Beebe, Lesile M., Takahashi, Tomoko, & Uliss-Weltz, Robin (1990). Pragmatic Transfer in ESL Refusals.In Scarcella, R. C., Anderson E., & Krashen, S. C. (Eds.), *On the Development of Communicative Comoetence in a Second Language* (pp. 55–73). New York: Newbury House.

Blum-Kulka, Shoshana, House, Juliane, & Kasper, Gabriele (1989). *Cross-Cultural Pragmatics: Request and Apologies*. Norwood, NJ: Ables.

Blum-Kulka, Shoshana (1982). Learning how to say what you mean in a second language: A study of the speech act performance of learners of Hebrew as a second language. *Applied Linguistics*, 3. pp. 29–59.

Blum-Kulka, Shoshana & Olshtain, Elite (1984). Requests and Apologies: A cross-cultural study of speech act realization patterns (CCSARP). *Applied Linguistic*, 5 (3). pp. 169–213.

Brown, Penelope & Levinson, Stephen (1987). *Politeness: Some universals in language usage*. Cambridge: Cambridge University Press.

Burke, Soyoung Baek (2010). *The construction of writing identity in the academic writing of Korean ESL students: A qualitative study of six Korean students in the U.S.* Unpublished doctoral dissertation, Indiana University of Pennsylvania.

Byon, Andrew Sangpil (2004). Sociopragmatic analysis of Korean requests: pedagogicalsettings. *Journal of Pragmatics*. 36. pp. 1673–1704.

Cherry, Roger (1988). Ethos vs. Persona: Self-representation in written discourse. *Written Communication*, 5(3), 251–276.

Cho, Nam Sung (1997). Kankokujin nihongogakushushano iraino bunmatsu hyogenni taisuru bunsekito hyoka [An analysis and evaluation of the request expressions at the end of a sentence of Korean Japanese language learners]. *Ilponeomunhak [Japanese literature]*, 3, pp. 93–111.

Connor, Ulla (1996). *Contrastive Rhetoric: Cross-cultural aspect of second-language writing*. Cambridge: Cambridge University Press.

Eggington, William, G. (1987). Written academic discourse in Korean: Implications for Effective communication. In U. Connor & R. B. Kaplan (Eds.), *Writing Across Languages: Analysis of L2 Text* (pp. 153–168). MA: Addison-Wesley.

Eom, Jeongmi (2001). Nihongoto kankokugono iiwakehyogenno taishokenkyu- Iraidanwano baai- [The comparative study of framings in Japanese and Korean language]. *Gengo bungaku kenkyu [Studies in language and literature]*. 20, 2. pp. 283–299.

Greenberg, Joseph H. (1974). *Language Typology: A Historical and Analytic Overview*. The Hague: Mouton.

Gumperz, John J. (1982). *Discourse Strategies*. Cambridge: Cambridge University Press.

Hall, Edward T. (1976). *Beyond Culture*. New York: Anchor Press.

Hinds, John (1983). Linguistics in written discourse in particular languages: Contrastive Studies: English and Japanese. In R.B. Kaplan (Ed.), *Annual Review of Applied Linguistics* (pp. 78–84). Rowley, MA: Newbury House.

Hinds, John (1987). Reader Versus Writer Responsibility: A New typology. In U. Connor & R. B. Kaplan (Eds.), *Writing Across Languages: Analysis of L2 Text* (pp. 141–152). MA: Addison-Wesley.

Hinds, John (1990). Inductive, Deductive, Quasi-inductive: Expository Writing in Japanese, Korean, Chinese, And Thai. In U. Connor and A. M. Johns (Eds.), *Coherence in Writing: Research and Pedagogical Perspectives Alexandria* (pp. 89–109), VA: Teachers of English to speaker of Other Languages Inc.

Hinkel, Eli (1997). Indirectness in L1 and L2 academic writing. *Journal of Pragmatics*, 27, pp. 361–386.

Hong, Minpyo (2006). Kanshato shazaihyogenno nikkanhikaku [A contrastive study of expressions of thank and apology between Japanese and Korean]. *Nihongogaku [Japanese linguistics]*. 25, 6. pp. 84–89.

Horie, Kaoru & Pardeshi, Prashant (2009). Gengono taiporozi: Ninchi ruikeronno apurochi [Language Typology: Approach to cognitive typology]. Tokyo: Kenkyusha.

Ichikawa, Takashi (1971). Kakidashiya musubino kakikata [The way of writings for introduction and conclusion]. In Inoue, Y. (Eds.), Sakubun shido jiten [Dictionary of writing education] (pp. 335–339). Daiichi hoki syuppan.

Ide, Risako (1998). 'Sorry for your kindness': Japanese interactional ritual in public discourse. *Journal of Pragmatic*, 29, pp. 509–529.

Ikeda, Rieko (1993). Shazaino taisho kenkyu: Nichibe taishokenkyu [A contrastive Study of apology: A contrastive study between Japanese and American]. *Nihongogaku [Japanese linguistics]*. 12, 12. pp. 13–21.

Ikegami, Yoshihiko (2000). *Nihongoroneno shotai [Invitation to Japanese Theory]*. Tokyo: Kodansha.

Inoue, Ippei (2003). Kontekusutokano sigentositeno kosho: gengoto komyunikeshonno setaigakueno siron [Address terms as Resources of Contextualization: Toward an Ecology of Language and Communication]. *Shakaigengokagaku [The Japanese Journal of Language in Society]*, 6(1). pp. 19–28.

Inoue, Ippei (2005). *Kotobano seitaikei: komyunikeshonwa nanide dekiteiruka [An ecological system of language: What consist of communication?]*. Yokohama: Keiogijukudaigaku syuppankai.

Jin, Sumi (2004). Nikkanniokeru shazaihyogenno ikkosatsu [A study of apology expressions in Japanese and Korean]. *Nihongo nihonbunka kenkyu [Studies of Japanese Language and culture]*, 14. pp. 23–35.

Kaplan, Robert B. (1966). Cultural thought patterns in inter-cultural education. *Language Learning*, 16. pp. 1–20.

Kawanari, Mika (1993). Iraihyogen [Express of request]. *Nihongogaku*, 12 (6). pp. 125–134.

Kim, Changnam (2006). Nihongoto kankokugono iraihyogenno shiyojittaini tsuite [The actual situation of use requests expression in Japanese and Korean]. *Ilpon munhwa hakpo [The Japanese culture]*, 31, pp. 23–42.

Kim, Inhwa & Maeda Tsunanori (1997). Bunshono koseniokeru nikkan taishokenkyu [A contrastive study of composition structure between Japanese and Korean] *Gaikokugo kyoikuronshu [Journal of foreign language]*, 19. pp. 419–435.

Kim, Jong Wan (2006). Iraihyogenno nikkanryogo taisho [A contrastive study of request expressions between Japanese and Korean]. *Kokubungakuchosa* [Investigation of Japanese],

18. pp. 251–261.
Kim, Jong Wan (2011). Ilboneo euiroihaengdongeui danhwagujomit Euiroipyohyeoneui teugjing: Ilbonin moeuohwaja hangugin, junggugin yuhagsaengeui gyoungwu [A Study on Discourse Structure and Expression of Japanese Requesting Behavior:Japanese Native Speakers, Korean and Chinese Students in Korea. *Ilponmunhwayenku [Study of Japanese culture]*, 37. pp.75–94.
Kim, Youngmi (1996). Ilponekyoyukuy kwancemeyse pon hankwukinuy kamsawa sacoyphyohyeney kwanhan kochal [The expressions of apology and Thank in Korean the view from Japanese education]. *Ileilmwunhak [Japanese language and literature]*, 6. pp.213–227.
Kobayashi, Hiroe (1984). *Rhetorical patterns in English and Japanese*. Unpublished doctoral dissertation, Colombia University Teachers College.
Kondo, Fumiko & Taniguchi, Hiromi (2007). A Comparative Study of Percetions of Apology Stategies between Japanese and Americans. *Gendai Syakaigaku [Modern Sociology]*, 9, pp. 131–154.
Kubota, Ryuko (1997). A reevaluation of the Uniqueness of Japanese Writing Discourse: Implications for Contrastive Rhetoric. *Writing communication*, 14 (4), pp. 460–480.
Kumagai, Tomoko & Shinozaki, Koichi (2006). Iraibamendeno hatarakikakekata niokeru sedaisa/chiikisa [The generation and regional gap in terms of the way encourage in requests]. In Kokuritsu kokugo kenkyuzyo (Eds.), *Gengokodo niokeru "hairyo"no syoso [Aspects of consideration with reference to language behavior]*, (pp. 19–54). Tokyo: Kurosiosyuppan.
Lai, Meili (2005). Irainiokeru owabi/shazaigata hyogenni kansuru kosatsu: Nihongo bogowashato taiwanjin nihongo gakushushawo taishoni [A Study of the Japanese Apology Expression in a Request: A Case of Native Speakers and Taiwanese Learners of Japanese]. *Waseda journal of Japanese applied linguistics*, 6, pp. 63–77.
Leech, Geoffrey N. (1980). *Explorations in semantics and pragmatics*. Amsterdam: John Benjamins.
Lee, Jung Min (2001). Bunsho kozono nikkantaishokenkyu: Shinbunshasetsuniokeru Kakidasio taishotosite [A contrastive Analysis of the Compositional Structures: In the Case of the Beginning Sentence in the Editorials in Japanese and Korean Newspapers]. *Ningenbunkato nihongokyoiku* [Human culture and Japanese education], 21, pp. 96–109.
Lee, Jung Min (2008). *Kannichi shinbun shasetsuniokeru shuchono sutoratezino taishokenkyu [A contrastive study on the strategy of insistence between Korean and Japanese editorials in newpapers]*. Tokyo: Hituzi syobo.
Leki, Ilona (1997). Cross-Talk: ESL issues and contrastive rhetoric. In C. Severino & J. E. Butler (Eds.), *Writing multicultural settings* (pp. 234–244). New York: Modern Language Association of America.
Levenston, Edward A. (1975). Aspects of testing the oral proficiency of adult immigrants to Canada. In L. Palmer & B. Spolsky (Eds.), *Paper on Language Testing 1967–1974*. Washington: TESOL.
Lim, Hyunjung & Tamaoka, Katsuo (2004). Kankokuno shokubadeno kosho siyono tekisetsuse handanni oyobosu zyokusei/taizinkankeitokusei/seikakutokuseino eikyo [Influence of characteristics, personalities and interpersonal factors on the appropriateness decisions of address-terms in the Korean workplace]. *Hiroshima keizaidaigaku kenkyuronsyu [Journal of Hiroshima University of Economics]*, 27 (1). pp. 29–44.

Lim, Hyunjung & Tamaoka, Katsuo (2010). Kankokugono koiyokyu hyogento sono hitehyogenno tenedoni kansuru kenkyu [The degree of politeness regarding a difference between affirmative and negative expressions for requests in Korean]. Yamaguchi kenritsudaigaku gakuzyutsu zyoho [Academic Archives of Yamaguchi Prefectural University], 3. pp. 11–23.

Matsuda, Yuichi, Kim, Yong Hee, Lee, Ju Eune, & Park, Eun Nam (2007). Kankokujin nihongo gakushushani mirareru puragumatikku toransufa: Irai bamenni okeru kankokugono seyuke "~Ja" no ekyoni tsuite [Pragmatic Transfer in Korean Learners of Japanese: The Influence of Korean -ja in Requests]. *Ibarakidaigaku ryugakusenta kiyo [Journal of the center of international students of Ibaraki University]*, 5. pp. 65–75.

Mauranen, Anna (1993). *Cultural differences in academic rhetoric*. Frankfurt am Main: Peter Lang.

Miyake, Misuzu (2007). *Contrastive Rhetoric in Japanese and English Writing –Refections on the History of Contrastive Rhetoric Studies, the Japanese Written Language, and its Educational System–*. Okayama: Fukuro Shuppan.

Mo, Eunyung (2001). Nikkanno iraihyogen [Request between Japanese and Korean]. *Kokubungakushiron [Japanese literary essay]*. 15. pp. 1–8.

Nam, Sangyoung (2009). Ilponeyseuy hanluwa hankuke kyoyuk [A Study on the 'Hallyu' and Education of Korean Language in Japan]. *Icyungenehak [Bilingual Research]*. 39. pp. 79–112.

Naotsuka, Reiko & Sakamoto, Nancy *et al.* (1981). *Mutual understanding of different cultures*. Tokyo: Taishukan.

Ogiwara, Chikako (2008). *Iisashi hatsuwano kaishakuriron: Kaiwa mokuteki tasse sukima ni yoru tenkai [Theory of interpretation of stop uttering: Development by schema of achievement the conversation's purpose]*. Tokyo: Shunpusha.

Ogoshi, Mariko (1993). Shazaino taisho kenkyu: Nikan taisho kenkyu [A contrastive study of apology: A contrastive study between Japanese and Korean]. *Nihongogaku [Japanese linguistics]*, 12. pp. 29–38.

Ogoshi, Mariko (1995). Iraihyogenno taisho kenkyu: Chosengono iraihyogen [A contrastive study of request: Request expression of Korean]. *Nihongogaku [Japanese linguistics]*, 14. pp. 50–59.

Oki, Hiroko, Kang, Suk-Woo, Zhao, Huamin, & Nishio, Junji (2009). Nikkanchuno gaigendanwanimiru hassoto hyogen [Japanese cultural attitudes and language viewed through external speech: A fundamental study of Japanese discourse and JSL]. *Jinbunkagakuronsyu [A collection of Human science studies]*. 44, pp. 1–25.

Ozaki, Yoshimitsu (2008). Iraikodoto kanshakodono nikkanhikaku [A comparative study of request and thank expressions between Japanese and Korean]. In Ozaki, Yoshimitsu. (Eds.), *Taijinkoodoo no nikkan taishoo kenkyuu:Gengo kodo no kite ni aru mono [A Contrastive Study of Communication Behavior in Japanese and Korean: Underlining Structures of Linguistic Behavior]*, (pp. 141–196). Tokyo: Hituzi Syobo.

Park, Tae-Hyon (2007). The Least You Should Know about Korean EFL Writers. *Sin Youngeoyoungmunhag [New English and English literature]*, 36, pp. 191–208.

Powers, John H. & Gong, Gwendolyn (1994). East Asian voice and the expression of cultural ethos. In K. B. Yancey (Ed.), *Voice on voice: Perspectives, definitions, inquiry* (pp. 202–225). Urbana, IL: National Council of Teachers of English.

Qi, Xiukun & Liu, Lida (2007). Differences between Reader/Writer Responsible Languages

Reflect in EFL Learner's Writing. *Intercultural Communication Studies*, XVI, pp. 148–159.
Sadanobu, Toshiyuki (2005). *Sasayaku koibito, rikimu repota [Whispering lovers, staining reporters]*. Tokyo: Iwanami Shoten.
Sasakawa, Yoko (1999). Ajia shakainiokeru poraitonesu (for you or for me) nitsuite: nihongo • kankokugo • chugokugo • taigo • indonesiagono hikaku [The politeness of request in Asian countries in terms of (for you or for me): Comparisons of Japanese, Korean, Chinese, Thai, and Indonesian]. *Shinwakokubun [Japanese literature of Shinwa]*. pp. 154–181.
Seo, Hong & Yanagisawa, Hiroya (2007). Nikkanno shinbunshasetsuniokeru taishoretorikku: Settokusenryakuno chigaiwo kangaeru [Contrastive rhetoric of editorials in Japanese and Korean newspaper]. *Hyogenkenkyu [Expression-formation Studies]*, 85, pp. 12–21.
Son, Mijung (2005). Iraidanwani arawareru keihyogenno shoso [An aspect of respect expressions in requests]. *Ilponemunhak [Japanese literature]*, 24. pp. 47–70.
Sugita, Kuniko (1994). Nihongo bogowashato nihongo gakushushano bunsho kozono tokucho: Bunhairetsu kadaini arawareta wadaino tenkai [The features of composition structures of Japanese native speakers and Japanese language learners –Development of issues appeared from sentence arrangement subject]. *Nihongo kyoiku [Japanese education]*, 84. pp. 14–26.
Swales, John M. (1990). *Genre analysis: English in academic and research settings*. New York: Cambridge University Press.
Takemata, Kazuo (1976). *Genko sippitsu nyumon [An introduction to writing manuscripts]*. Tokyo: Natsumesha.
Takigawa, Yuzuru (2006). Misunderstandings in Intercultural Communication: Different Strategy in Making the point in a story Between Japanese and Americans. *Osakajogakuindaigakukiyo* [Memoirs of Osaka-Jogakuin-University], 3, pp. 15–23.
Tao, Lin (2007). The Construction of Semantic Formulas on Apologizing Expressions in Chinese. *Ningenshakaikankyo kenkyu [Human-Socio Environment Studies]*, 14, pp. 19–38.
Tsuchida, Kazumi (2003). Nihonjin gakuseito kankokujin ryugakusei niokeru iraino danwa sutoratezi tsukaiwakeno bunseki: Goyoronteki poraitonesuno kantenkara [An analysis of request strategy between Japanese native speakers and Korean Japanese learners: The view from pragmatics]. *Koidekinen nihonkyoikukenkyu kaironbunsyu [The collected introductions in Japanese education of memorial of Koide]*, 11, pp.41–54.
Usami, Mayumi (2002). *Discourse Politeness in Japanese Conversation: Some Implications for a Universal Theory of Politeness*. Tokyo: Hituzi Syobo.
Wada, Yurie, Horie, Kaoru, & Yoshimoto Akira. (2010). Iraihyogenniokeru nihongogakushushano chukangengo: Chugokugobogowasha kankokugo bogowashano bogoteni: [The middle language of Japanese language learners in terms of request expressions –Influence of native languages of Chinese and Korean learners]. *Tohokudaigaku kotokyoikukaihatsu senta kiyo [Journal of center for the Advancement of Higher Education of Tohoku University]*, 5, pp. 171–177.
Yamane, Chie (2002). *Nihongono danwani okeru fira [Fillers in Japanese discourse]*. Tokyo: Kurosio Syuppan.
Yamamoto, Motoko (2003). Kanshano shazaihyogen 'sumimasen'; 'sumimasen'ga kanshato shazaino ryohono imio motsuwak [Two meaning of "Sumimasen": Apologies and Thanks. *Shinshudaigaku ryugakusenta kiyo [Journal of International Student Center, Shinshu University]*, 4, pp. 1–13.

Yim, Youngcheol (2003). Nihonjintono komyunikeishyon [Communication with Japanese people]. *Sahoieoneohag [Socio-Linguistics]*, pp. 239–251.

Yim, Youngcheol & Ide, Risako (2004). *Hashito chokkarak: Kotobato bunkano nikkan hikaku. [Chopstick and chopstick: Comparison of the language and culture between Japanese and Korean].* Tokyo: Taishukanshoten.

Yoo, Hye-jung (2008). Kannichino iraidanwaniokeru storatejino tsukaiwake: Irai sheiritsu no maeto ushirotono hikakuwo chushinni [A Comparative Study of the Strategy of Request Discourse of Korean and Japanese]. *Ilbon munhwa yeongu [Studies on Japanese culture]*, 28, pp. 157–177.

Yoon, Sumi (2008). Comparison between Korean and Japanese address terms as a contextualization husband-wife's dialogue. *Inquiries into Korean Linguistics*, 3, pp. 377–387.

Yoon, Sumi (2009). A Contrastive Study of Metacommunicative Functions of Address Terms between Husband and Wife in Korea and Japan. *Current Issues in Unity and Diversity of Languages: Collection of the Papers Selected from the International Congress of Linguists (CIL)*, 18, pp. 3819–3831.

Appendices

Appendix 1　The DCT written in Japanese

言葉の使い方についての調査

　私は金沢大学大学院人間社会環境研究科博士後期課程で社会言語学を研究しているユン秀美と申します。以下のアンケートは、私の博士論文の資料としてのみ用いるもので、他の目的には一切使用しません。ご協力をよろしくお願いします。

　このアンケートは、大学生が用いる言葉について調べることを目的としています。以下の様々な会話の場面で、あなたはどのような言い方をしますか。あなたの言い方で発話文を書いてください(説明文で説明をするのではなく<u>話し言葉で書いてください</u>)。

出身地：(　　　　　　　　)　　現在の居住地：(　　　　　　　　　)
年齢：(　　　　　　才　)　　性別：(　男性　・　女性　)
専攻分野：(　　　　　　　　　　)

1. あなたは親しい友達と一緒に映画を見ることになっています。しかし、待ち合わせしている映画館前に、20分ほど遅れて着きました。

あなた：( )
友達　：大丈夫、授業が長引いたのなら仕方ないよ。
あなた：( )
友達　：チケット？　もう二人分買ってあるよ。
あなた：( )
友達　：映画のチケットぐらいでお礼を言わなくてもいいよ。

2. あなたは受講する講義のレポートを出しに直接、担当教員の研究室に行きました。しかし、先生は締め切りが過ぎたので受けとることができないと言います。

先生　：レポートの締め切りはおとといまでだったんですが。
あなた：（　　　　　　　　　　　　　　　　　　　　　　　　　）
先生　：いいえ、謝らなくてもいいです。
あなた：（　　　　　　　　　　　　　　　　　　　　　　　　　）
先生　：頼まれても原則を守らないと他の学生と不平等になるので、受け取ることはできません。

　　　　　　　　　　　　　　　　　　　　　ご協力ありがとうございます。

Appendix 2　The DCT written in Korean

말의 사용에 관한 조사

　저는 일본 가나자와대학 대학원 인간사회환경연구과 박사후기 과정에서 사회언어학을 연구하고 있는 윤수미라고 합니다. 아래의 앙케이트는 제 박사논문 자료로만 사용되며 다른 목적으로는 사용하지 않을 것을 약속드립니다. 협조를 부탁합니다.
　이 앙케이트의 목적은 대학생이 사용하는 말에 대해 조사하는 것입니다. 아래에 제시되어 있는 다양한 대화 장면에서 당신은 어떻게 말을 합니까? 당신의 자연스러운 어투로 대화문을 적어주세요 (설명문으로 설명을 하는 것이 아니라 당신이 말하는 말투 그대로 적어주세요).

출신지: (　　　　　　　　　) 현재 주거지: (　　　　　　　　　　　)
연령: (　　만　　　　　세) 성별: (남 ・ 여)
전공 분야: (　　　　　　　　　)

1. 당신은 친한 친구와 함께 영화를 보기로 했습니다. 그러나 약속 장소인 영화관에 20분 정도 늦게 도착했습니다.

| 당신 : (　　　　　　　　　　　　　　　　　　　　　　) |
| 친구 : 괜찮아 수업이 늦게 끝났으니까 어쩔 수 없지. |
| 당신 : (　　　　　　　　　　　　　　　　　　　　　　) |
| 친구 : 티켓? 벌써 2장 사 놨어. |
| 당신 : (　　　　　　　　　　　　　　　　　　　　　　) |
| 친구 : 영화 표 정도로 인사 안 해도 돼. |

2. 당신은 수강하고 있는 강의의 레포트를 제출하기 위하여 직접 담당 교수님의 연구실에 갔습니다. 그러나 교수님은 마감 시간이 지났으므로 받을 수가 없다고 말하고 있습니다.

> 교수 : 레포트 마감 기한은 그저께까지 였습니다.
> 당신 : (   )
> 교수 : 아니 사과는 하지 않아도 돼요.
> 당신 : (   )
> 교수 : 그렇게 부탁해도 받을 수 없습니다. 원칙을 지키지 않으면 다른 학생들과 불공평하게 됩니다.

협조해 주서서 감사합니다.

Appendix 3　The questionnaire written in Japanese

言葉の使い方についての調査

　私は金沢大学大学院人間社会環境研究科博士後期課程で社会言語学を研究しているユン秀美と申します。以下のアンケートは、私の博士論文の資料としてのみ用い、他の目的には一切使用しませんので、ご協力をよろしくお願いします。

　このアンケートは、職場でよく用いる言葉について調べることを目的としています。以下の職場での様々な会話の場面で、あなたはどのような言い方をしますか。あなたの言い方で発話文を書いてください(説明文で説明をするのではなく話し言葉で書いてください)。ご協力をよろしくお願いいたします。

出身地：(　　　　　　　　　)　　現在の居住地：(　　　　　　)
年齢：(　　　　　　才　)　　性別：(　男性　・　女性　)
学歴：(　　　　　　卒　)　　結婚：(　既婚　・　未婚　)
職業：(　　　　　　　　　)

1. あなたは以下の相手と二人で打ち合わせをすることになっています。しかし、あなたはその打ち合わせに10分ほど遅れてしまいました。相手が以下の三人の場合、それぞれの相手にどう言いますか。

1-1：相手が上司の場合
(　　　　　　　　　　　　　　　　　　　　　　　　　　　)
1-2：相手が同期の場合
(　　　　　　　　　　　　　　　　　　　　　　　　　　　)
1-3：相手が部下の場合
(　　　　　　　　　　　　　　　　　　　　　　　　　　　)

2. あなたは今日とても忙しく昼ごはんを食べに行く時間がありません。既に

食事をしてきた以下の人が近くのコンビニに行くと言います。ついでにあなたのサンドイッチを買ってきて欲しい時、相手が以下の三人の場合、あなたはそれぞれの相手に対してどう言いますか。

2-1：相手が上司の場合
(　　　　　　　　　　　　　　　　　　　　　　　　　)
2-2：相手が同期の場合
(　　　　　　　　　　　　　　　　　　　　　　　　　)
2-3：相手が部下の場合
(　　　　　　　　　　　　　　　　　　　　　　　　　)

　　　　　　　　　　　　　　　ご協力ありがとうございます。

Appendix 4   The questionnaire written in Korean

말의 사용에 관한 조사

저는 일본 가나자와대학 대학원 인간사회환경 연구과 박사후기과정에서 사회언어학을 연구하고 있는 윤수미라고 합니다. 아래의 앙케이트는 제 박사논문 자료로만 사용되며 다른 목적으로는 사용하지 않을 것을 약속드립니다. 협조를 부탁합니다.

이 앙케이트의 목적은 직장에서 자주 사용하는 말에 대해 조사하는 것입니다. 아래에 제시되어 있는 다양한 대화 장면에서 당신은 어떻게 말을 합니까? 당신의 자연스러운 어투로 대화문을 적어주세요(설명문으로 설명을 하는 것이 아니라 당신이 말하는 말투 그대로 적어주세요).

출신지: (   )   현재 주거지: (   )
연령: (만   세)   성별: (남 · 여)
학력: (졸)   결혼: (기혼 · 미혼)
직업: (   )

1. 당신은 아래의 상대와 둘이서 회의를 하기로 했습니다. 그러나 당신은 그 회의에 10분 정도 늦었습니다. 상대가 아래의 3명(상사, 동기, 부하)인 경우, 각각 어떻게 말을 합니까?

1-1: 상대가 상사인 경우
(   )
1-2: 상대가 동기인 경우
(   )
1-3: 상대가 부하의 경우
(   )

2. 당신은 오늘 매우 바빠서 점심을 먹으러 갈 시간도 없습니다. 먼저 점심을 먹고 온 아래의 사람이 근처에 있는 편의점에 간다고 말합니다. 가는 길에 당신에게 샌드위치를

사 주기를 바랄 때, 아래의 3명(상사, 동기, 부하)에게 각각 어떻게 말합니까?

2-1: 상대가 상사인 경우
(   )
2-2: 상대가 동기인 경우
(   )
2-3: 상대가 부하의 경우
(   )

협조해 주서서 감사합니다.

Index

a
acquisition of Japanese as a second language 22
age and status 80
address terms as contextualization cues 50, 62
alerters 90
Anglo-American 10
author's intention 16

b
Blum-Kulka 28
Brown and Levinson 28

c
Classifying Typology 7
close friend 75
Cognitive Typology 8
comparative writing patterns 12
Connor 10
contextualization cues 2
conversational partners 68
convey the emotion 49

d
defense 44, 62
delayed introduction of purpose 11, 61
difference in attitudes to face 47
different social groups 80
discourse politeness 92

e
East Asian languages 12
editorials 18
efficient foreign language teaching 64
Eggington 10, 15
ESL or EFL writing pedagogy 16
experimental conversations 23
explanations for apology 44
expository prose 14
expressions of apology 44
expressions of apology and thanks 48

f
face-threatening acts 18, 28
Finnish 10
framework 90
functions of interjections 74

g
Generalizing Typology 7
globalization 1
GS pattern 14
Gumperz 2

h
helpful information for interlocutors 77
high-context culture 11
higher status or older person 76
Hinds 2, 8
honorific systems 75

i
IFID 74
iiwake 62, 91
imperative 21
indirectness strategies 13
Individualizing Typology 7
influence of daily use of english 39, 42, 44, 50
intercultural communication 1
interpersonal consideration 92
interrogative 21
intimate person 22
intrusive subjects 89

j
Japanese compositions 13
Japanese husbands 24

k
Kileki appa (goose father) 17
Korean husbands 24
Korean social convention 76
Korean Wave 1

l
language typology 2
lower status person 76

m
MCT (Multiple Comparison Test) 55
military service 30
mutual ground 23

n
negative strategies 61

o

offer of repair   75
Ogoshi   19

p

personal pronouns   16
person of higher position   89
polite explanation   47, 62
positive strategies   61, 91
Pragmatic politeness   93
preface to a request   90
proper expressions   23
psychological facts   91

q

qualitative analysis   33
quantitative analysis   32
quasi-inductive   11

r

reader/listener-responsible   8
recommendation situations   23
relationship between the speaker and listener   75
rhetorical pattern Japanese essays   9
Ryan's method   55

s

semantic formulas   33
sentence types   88
SG pattern   14
social structures   48
speaker's face   28
speaker's features   96
speaker's gender   77
spoken discourse   3
state their real purpose in earlier turns   95
statistical analyses   33
subordinate conjunctions   18

t

Tensei Jingo   9
typical word for compliment   48

v

verbal realizations   33
vertical social-cultural structure (tate shakai)   47

w

writer/speaker-responsible   8
written discourse   3

【著者紹介】

尹 秀美（ユン スゥミ）

1980年韓国釜山生まれ。
韓国東亜大学校中国・日本学部日語日文学科卒業。
金沢大学大学院人間社会環境研究科博士課程修了。博士（文学）。
現在、金沢大学男女共同参画キャリアデザインラボラトリー博士研究員、金沢大学非常勤講師（朝鮮語担当）。

〈主な著書・論文〉
"A Contrastive Study of Metacommunicative Functions of Address Terms between Husband and Wife in Korea and Japan" (*Current Issues in Unity and Diversity of Languages*, The 18th International Congress of Linguists (CIL), 2009), "Who is Responsible for Understanding in a Conversation?: A Contrastive Pragmatic Analysis of Utterances in Japanese and Korean" (*Indian Journal of Applied Linguistics* (IJAL), 37, 2012) など。

Hituzi Linguistics in English No. 22

A Contrastive Study of Responsibility for Understanding Utterances between Japanese and Korean

発行　2014年2月14日　初版1刷
定価　8400円＋税
著者　© 尹秀美
発行者　松本功
印刷所　株式会社 ディグ
製本所　株式会社 中條製本工場
発行所　株式会社 ひつじ書房
　　　〒112-0011 東京都文京区千石2-1-2 大和ビル2F
　　　Tel.03-5319-4916　Fax.03-5319-4917
　　　郵便振替 00120-8-142852
　　　toiawase@hituzi.co.jp　http://www.hituzi.co.jp/

ISBN978-4-89476-685-3　C3080

造本には充分注意しておりますが、落丁・乱丁などがございましたら、小社かお買上げ書店にておとりかえいたします。ご意見、ご感想など、小社までお寄せ下されば幸いです。

Hituzi Linguistics in English

No. 18 fMRI Study of Japanese Phrasal Segmentation:
Neuropsychological Approach to Sentence Comprehension
大嶋秀樹著　定価 15000 円+税

No. 19 Typological Studies on Languages in Thailand and Japan
宮本正夫・小野尚之・Kingkarn Thepkanjana・上原聡編　定価 9000 円+税

No. 20 Repetition, Regularity, Redundancy:
Norms and Deviations of Middle English Alliterative Meter
守屋靖代著　定価 13000 円+税

No. 21 A Cognitive Pragmatic Analysis of Nominal Tautologies
山本尚子著　定価 8800 円+税